THROW AWAY YOUR RAPTURE RUG!

What Father God Is Waiting for

PATRICIA KOALSKA

outskirts
press

Throw Away Your Rapture Rug!
What Father God is Waiting for
All Rights Reserved.
Copyright © 2022 Patricia Koalska
v2.0

The opinions expressed in this manuscript are solely the opinions of the author and do not represent the opinions or thoughts of the publisher. The author has represented and warranted full ownership and/or legal right to publish all the materials in this book.

This book may not be reproduced, transmitted, or stored in whole or in part by any means, including graphic, electronic, or mechanical without the express written consent of the publisher except in the case of brief quotations embodied in critical articles and reviews.

Outskirts Press, Inc.
http://www.outskirtspress.com

ISBN: 978-1-9772-5569-3

Cover photo belongs to the author Patricia Koalska. All rights reserved. Used with permission.

The Bible verses are from The Amplified Version (AMP) unless otherwise stated. Take from the Bible Gateway website.

Outskirts Press and the "OP" logo are trademarks belonging to Outskirts Press, Inc.

PRINTED IN THE UNITED STATES OF AMERICA

DEDICATION

To my Father God.

You are absolutely good. You are The LORD, the LORD God. You are compassionate and gracious, slow to anger, and abounding in loving kindness and faithfulness. You keep mercy and loving kindness for thousands, forgiving iniquity and transgression and sin. You are patient and kind. You do not envy. You do not boast. You are not proud. You are not rude. You are not self seeking. You are not easily angered. You give no record of wrongs. You rejoice with the truth. You always protect, always trust, always hope, always persevere. My Father God you never fail. You deserve all the glory, the honor and adoration.

To The LORD Jesus Christ.

You are the One my heart is set on. The Book of Revelation is The Revelation of Jesus Christ, the whole Bible is the revelation of Jesus Christ. You are Alpha and Omega. You are Heaven's treasure. You are the creator of everything. You are eternal. You are the Word, You are the mystery of the ages. You are the redeemer of mankind. You are holy, perfect and pure. You are Priest and King, You are wonderful counselor, mighty God, everlasting Father, Prince of peace. Thank you for continually praying for me and for singing over me.

To Holy Spirit.

You are my Friend, my Comforter, my Advocate, my Intercessor, my Counselor, my Strengthener, my Standby, my Teacher, my Guide. You will forever be with me. Tank you for helping me write this book, I would have not done it without you.

LORD God Almighty, I love you.

To Ron, my beloved husband and the love of my life. I love your talents and creativity, your silly sense of humor and your childlike view of life, your wisdom and inner peace. Thank you for teaching me to not run around all over the place accomplishing little, but doing a little every day to accomplish much. You are my heaven sent gift.

To Cristina Anderson, Jose and Randy Reyna, and Brenda Quimby. I soooo look forward to being with you every Wednesday morning. Thank you for allowing me to go over this book with you and for your input to make it clearer to understand. Your friendship and love means the world to me. I love you all.

ACKNOWLEDGMENTS

A BIG THANK YOU

To Kat Kerr the Revelator for inspiring the blueprint for this book. Listening to you Revealing Heaven has made me fall in love with Jesus even more. Wohoo!!

To Paul Keith Davis, teacher and prophet, your Voice of the Bride webinars 7 through 18 on the Book of Revelation gave me insight about interpreting the times we live in now.

To Kevin Zadai, for the gems of revelation you drop off every time you speak, especially about discerning the times. I love every minute I have spent studying with you at Warrior Notes School of Ministry. I'm excited to get my next degree in Bible and Theology!

To Lance Wallnau, business man, teacher and prophet. I am inspired, enlightened and delighted by your energetic almost humorous yet profound approach to the ways of God's Kingdom living. Let's take the nations for Jesus as His inheritance!!

AMONG THE CLOUD OF WITNESSES:

To Madame Jeanne Guyon, your passionate love for Jesus is a road map for me to follow Him who is worthy. You are an example of what it looks like to be a revealed daughter of the Most High even in times of utmost darkness.

To Neville Johnson, a delightful teacher, prophet and revelator of God's mysteries. I still have so much to learn from you, thank you for the audio recordings and videos of the message God entrusted you.

To Kenneth E Hagin, your teachings about the Authority of the Believer, the Holy Spirit and the role of the church on earth have given me understanding of what the mature sons of God should look like. Your testimony of your walk with God makes me want a much closer relationship with the LORD.

TABLE OF CONTENTS

Preface		I
Chapter 1	The Signs of the Times and of the End of the Age	1
Chapter 2	The Great Commission	12
Chapter 3	The Bride Makes Herself Ready	22
Chapter 4	The Unity of the Faith	29
Chapter 5	They Will Be Known For Their Love For Each Other	44
Chapter 6	The Jews Will Be Provoked To Jealousy	53
Chapter 7	The Manifestation of the Sons of God	70
Chapter 8	The Greater Works	85
Chapter 9	The Earth Will Be Filled With The Knowledge Of The Glory Of The Lord	99
Chapter 10	The Powers Of The Age To Come	120
Chapter 11	Possessing the Land and the Feast of Tabernacles	153

PREFACE

From the day I was born again in Jesus Christ in 1995 and started reading and studying the Bible, I was curious about "the end times" but I wondered why everyone was so focused on God's enemy and the doom and gloom instead of focusing on God Himself and His wonderful works.

It was until the 2010s that I started hearing some people address some of the Last Days signs from Heaven's perspective but I haven't found a book that talks about them, so I decided to write it myself.

The end of this age, the taking away of the saints, and the second coming of the Lord Jesus Christ are not determined by the works of the evil one but by the works of the Holy Spirit through the Body of Messiah Jesus.

The LORD God Almighty knows absolutely everything, He says: *"For My thoughts are not your thoughts, Nor are your ways My ways," declares the* LORD. *"For as the heavens are higher than the earth, So are My ways higher than your ways And My thoughts higher than your thoughts Isaiah 55:8-9*, but He reveals His secrets to His servants the prophets (Amos 3:7), and they wrote it for the people to know and to understand. Jesus wept over Jerusalem because the people didn't discern their time of visitation (Luke 19:44). In Matthew 16:1-3 and Luke 12:54-56 Jesus remarks that the religious Jews could not interpret the signs of the times; they knew the prophecies about Messiah but they didn't recognize Him when He came.

The tribe of Issachar had an anointing to discern the times to know what to do: *Of the tribe of Issachar, men who understood the times, with knowledge of what Israel should do. 1 Chron 12:32a*

It is a legitimate desire to ask Father God for an anointing to understand the times and to have the knowledge to know what to do. God shows no partiality, with Him one person is not more important than another (Rom 2:11).

Even though God has the power to do everything by Himself, he chose to send His Holy Spirit to help and empower the Body of Christ to defeat His enemy, to make His kingdom come and to do His will on earth as it is in heaven.

Every chapter in this book is worth a book in itself but for the sake of space I only touch the surface of each subject.

I do not mention the translated name for hillel (Isaiah 14:12) or any of his names, but instead I use "the evil one" or "God's enemy", because his name is not worthy of mention, neither it's worthy to be capitalized.

In this book you will find the scriptures that have not been fulfilled yet hence Father God can not send Jesus back. *So will My word be which goes out of My mouth; It will not return to Me void (useless, without result), Without accomplishing what I desire, And without succeeding in the matter for which I sent it. Isaiah 55:11.*

CHAPTER 1

THE SIGNS OF THE TIMES AND OF THE END OF THE AGE

Tell us… What will be the sign of Your coming and of the end (completion, consummation) of the age? Matt 24:3b.

Even though Jesus' disciples didn't understand Jesus actual mission in Israel, they knew He was the Messiah, the Savior, the Son of God, and the fulfillment of prophecies about Jesus spoken in times past. They had heard Jesus talk about interpreting the times and about being capable of "missing the time of visitation". They had heard Jesus talk about "leaving them and going to where He couldn't be found". I can see the disciples minds spinning around trying to grasp Jesus words and teachings. Didn't the prophecies say Jesus was supposed to become king, to sit on the throne of David, to become the deliverer of Israel? Yet Jesus was talking about being betrayed by one of his friends, being delivered into the hands of his enemies, being crucified and... coming back after three days. Then, when Jesus came back He said he had to leave again and he would come back later but He didn't know when.

The disciples asked Jesus this very important question: "What will be the sign of Your coming and of the end of the age?"

Jesus listed a bunch of doom and gloom events but ended up saying:

See that you are not frightened, for those things must take place, **but that is not yet the end** *[of the age]. Matt 24:6b.*

But all these things are merely the beginning of birth pangs [of the intolerable anguish and the time of unprecedented trouble]. Matt 24:8.

When you hear of wars and rumors of wars, do not be alarmed (frightened, troubled); these things must take place, **but the end is not yet.** *For nation will rise up against nation, and kingdom against kingdom; there will be earthquakes in various places; there will be famines. These things are the beginning of the birth pangs [the intolerable anguish and suffering]. Mark 13:7-8.*

When you hear of wars and disturbances [civil unrest, revolts, uprisings], do not panic; for these things must take place first, **but the end will not come immediately.** *" Luke 21:9.*

According to this, Jesus was saying "Look guys, the earthquakes, famines, wars, pestilences, signs in the heavens, etc, are like birth pangs, but it's not the delivery time yet. When the delivery time actually comes it will be incredibly more terrifying".

Then Jesus stated what would be one of the actual signs of His next coming and of the end of the age. Mind you that this is about the end of an age. Nobody was talking about the end of the world or the end of man kind. An age is a period of time where certain things happen, like the dark age (from about 476 AD to 1000 AD). Jesus said:

This good news of the kingdom [the gospel] will be preached throughout the whole world as a testimony to all the nations, **and then the end [of the age] will come**. *Matt 24:14.*

The gospel of God's kingdom must be preached throughout the whole world as a testimony to all the nations. Note it is "the gospel of the **kingdom**" not only the gospel of salvation. Salvation or the born again experience is what transforms a person from spiritually dead to alive and makes him/her God's son/daughter. The gospel of God's kingdom was the focus of Jesus teachings on earth and what He taught about after His resurrection. Remember many of his parables started with "the kingdom of heaven is like". Understanding the way heaven is and operates is of utmost importance for the believer in Jesus Christ. First of all as the believer in Christ learns the principles of the kingdom of heaven, and starts living according to those principles, transformation starts to happen and starts to operate more like Jesus. Even though Jesus had not been crucified and resurrected yet, He operated in the kingdom of heaven's ways empowered by the Holy Spirit. Jesus mission on earth at that time was to ransom mankind. The absolute purpose of the Word becoming flesh was to become God's sacrificial lamb that would reconcile mankind with Almighty God and turning the hearts of a rebellious people to a loving Father. He left us example of what it looks like to be like Father God and to live by the kingdom of heaven's ways so that we could fulfill the great commission and to do greater works than what He did.

Let's also remember that at the outpouring or baptism in the Holy Spirit, the apostle Peter gave his famous sermon:

this is [the beginning of] what was spoken of through the prophet Joel:

*'AND IT SHALL BE **IN THE LAST DAYS**,' says God, 'THAT I WILL POUR OUT MY SPIRIT UPON ALL MANKIND; AND YOUR SONS AND YOUR DAUGHTERS SHALL PROPHESY, AND YOUR YOUNG MEN SHALL SEE [divinely prompted] VISIONS, AND YOUR OLD MEN SHALL DREAM [divinely prompted] DREAMS; EVEN ON MY BOND-SERVANTS, BOTH MEN AND WOMEN, I WILL IN THOSE DAYS POUR OUT MY SPIRIT And they shall prophesy. 'AND I WILL BRING ABOUT WONDERS IN THE SKY ABOVE AND SIGNS (attesting miracles) ON THE EARTH BELOW, BLOOD AND FIRE AND SMOKING VAPOR. 'THE SUN SHALL BE TURNED INTO DARKNESS AND THE MOON INTO BLOOD, BEFORE THE GREAT AND GLORIOUS DAY OF THE LORD COMES. 'AND IT SHALL BE THAT EVERYONE WHO CALLS UPON THE NAME OF THE LORD [invoking,*

adoring, and worshiping the Lord Jesus] SHALL BE SAVED (rescued spiritually).' Acts 2:17-21.

Around the time when Jesus went through Calvary, was crucified, died, was buried, preached in Abraham's Bosom (Paradise), and preached in hell; a Red Blood Moon was happening, and a solar eclipse when He died. These signs in the heavens were right before "The Great and Glorious Day of the Lord" when Father God sent Holy Spirit to raise Jesus from the death. The graves of many of the saints of old were open, those saints came back to life and walked on the streets of Jerusalem talking to people. Those that had seen this magnificent event from afar in a foretelling way, and made provision for their bones to be buried in that place, had positioned themselves with the hope to see The Great and Glorious Day of the Lord. They did.

Peter was saying in that famous first sermon: "Hey guys, This is That. It's the beginning of the last days". So, the last days started over 2,000 years ago, in which the world has experienced all the things Jesus talked about, except that the Gospel of the kingdom has not been preached throughout all the earth. Even in the massive evangelistic crusades where millions of people are being born again, they are not being taught the Gospel of the Kingdom, the nations are not being discipled. The church has been making converts but very few are making disciples.

Many years later the apostle Paul was given revelation by Jesus Christ Himself (Gal 1:12) about the signs of the times (among many other things). He wrote to the church in Thessalonica:

But you, believers, [all you who believe in Christ as Savior and acknowledge Him as God's Son] are not in spiritual darkness [nor held by its power], that the day [of judgment] would overtake you [by surprise] like a thief; for you are all sons of light and sons of day. We do not belong to the night nor to darkness. 1 Thess 5:4-5.

Paul was pretty much saying: 'look guys, because you are born again and you are not in the dark, the coming of Jesus should not take you by surprise". The glorious church ought to wait for Him with the lamps and the oil ready, always with the ears tuned in to the sound of the last trumpet. Then he wrote more about it encouraging the brethren to not be alarmed or easily unset by some prophecy, report or anything else, reminding them that he had personally talked to them about these things.

*Do you not remember that when I was still with you, I was telling you these things? And you know what restrains him now [from being revealed]; it is so that he will be revealed at his own [appointed] time. For the mystery of lawlessness [rebellion against divine authority and the coming reign of lawlessness] is already at work; [**but it is restrained**] only until he who now restrains it is taken out of the way. 2 Thess 2:5-7.*

Here Paul states there's "a restrainer" that, as long as it is on earth, the son of perdition will not be revealed and the lawless one is restrained or kept at bay. Remember that the Restrainer are the Holy Spirit and the faithful remnant. When we look at the scriptures closely, the evil one should only be allowed three and a half years to do whatever he wants, the rest of the time "the restrainer (the triumphant church)" should not give him any room to operate. Paul wrote a lot about the ways of the kingdom of God and the power and authority of the believers in Christ to overcome the evil one, just as Jesus said that the gates of hell will not prevail over His church that is set on Him (the rock, the cornerstone, the foundation). As of 2022 it is very clear that the gates of hell ARE prevailing over Christ's church. Will God's Word come back to Him void?

In Acts 1:6-8a we read: *So when they had come together, they asked Him repeatedly, "Lord, are You at this time reestablishing the kingdom and restoring it to Israel?" He said to them, "It is not for you to know the times or epochs which the Father has fixed by His own authority. But you will receive power and ability when the Holy Spirit comes upon you;*

Even after Jesus resurrection the disciples didn't understand God's ways and plan. The mystery of the ages (the whole plan of salvation through Jesus, the reconciliation to Father God, etc) had not been unveiled to them yet, it was the duty of the Holy Spirit to show and to teach them all that. Later on the apostle Paul explains to the church about the times and epochs revealed then by Holy Spirit and by Jesus Himself.

Through the Holy Spirit, Jesus gave the church all power and all authority over all the power of the enemy. Father God made His Holy Spirit available to His children who want Him, to help , teach, guide, counsel, and empower them, etc. The church with the help of Holy Spirit are "the restrainer" Paul talks about. As long as they are on the earth, the three and a half years of tribulation will not happen. That doesn't mean that the evil one will not try to change the times and the seasons and to try to make things happen before his time, because he really doesn't know either when that time will actually be. Every century, the evil one has groomed and empowered people to take over the world and to fulfill his agenda, and every time he has done much damage, but in the end he has been defeated and he has to start all over again. Every time, the faithful remnant who has been led of the Holy Spirit has overcome. And again creation has the opportunity to be liberated from its bondage to decay and to be brought into the glorious freedom of the children of God. (Rom 8:18-26).

The Gospel of the Kingdom must be preached to all the world and the nations need to be discipled in the ways of God's kingdom. Then, the end of this age will happen, and another age will come as the apostle Paul reveals:

*He made known to us the mystery of His will according to His good pleasure, which He purposed in Christ, with regard to the fulfillment of the times [**that is, the end of history, the climax of the ages**]—to bring all things together in Christ, [both] things in the heavens and things on the earth. Eph 1:9-10.*

These are in accordance with the working of His mighty strength which He produced in Christ when He raised Him from the dead and seated Him (Jesus) at His (Father God) own right hand in the heavenly places, far above all rule and authority and power and dominion [whether angelic or human], and [far above] every name that is named [above every title that can be conferred], **not only in this age and world but also in the one to come.** *Eph 1:19b-21.*

There are at least two more ages to look forward to: One will be the Kingdom Age.

In 2012 several prophets of the Most High God declared that Christ's church had stepped through the threshold to the next season (age). This was from the Church Age to the Kingdom age. Jesus' prayer "Your kingdom come Your will be done **on earth** as it is in heaven" has the intention to bring God's ways and government to the earth, just at it is in heaven. If it wasn't possible Jesus would not have told us to pray for it. This "climax of the ages" or threshold has come like birth pangs where everything that can be shaken IS being shaken. God is judging, exposing and burning everything. At the end of the shaking those who laid a foundation other than the one which is already laid, which is Jesus Christ, that is to say those believers who built on the foundation with gold, silver, precious stones, wood, hay, straw, each one's work will be clearly shown for what it is; for this day of judgment will disclose it, because it is being revealed with fire, and the fire is testing the quality *and* character *and* worth of each person's work. If any person's work which he has built on this foundation, that is, any outcome of his effort remains and survives this test, he will receive a reward as part of the remnant. But if any person's work is burned up by the test, the believer will suffer the loss of his reward; yet he himself will be saved, but only as one who has barely escaped through fire. This shaking of all things includes governments, academia, arts and entertainment, family, religion, finances, and media. Their foundations are being exposed and burnt so that the Kingdom Age will start with a clear page, no wicked structure will be allowed to enter in. Only the things which cannot be shaken may remain.

We don't know how long the Kingdom Age will last, but it will be a great time for the earth and it's inhabitants.

The body of Christ will be on the earth when the mark of the beast will be set in motion, hence the warning to not take the mark, but the Holy Spirit and the bride of Christ will be taken away right before the actual antichrist is revealed.

The other age to look forward to will be at the end of the Kingdom Age, and it will start after the taking away of Holy Spirit and the Bride for the Lamb's marriage in heaven, which will last the same time of the great tribulation on the earth.

...and bound the evil one [securely] for a thousand years (a millennium); and the angel hurled him into the abyss, and closed it and sealed it above him [preventing his escape or rescue], so that he would no longer deceive and seduce the nations, until

the thousand years were at an end. After these things he must be liberated for a short time.

*And then I saw thrones, and sitting on them were those to whom judgment [that is, the authority to act as judges] was given. And I saw the souls of those who had been beheaded because of their testimony of Jesus and because of the word of God, and those who had refused to worship the beast or his image, and had not accepted his mark on their forehead and on their hand; and they came to life **and reigned with Christ for a thousand years**. The rest of the dead [the non-believers] did not come to life again until the thousand years were completed. This is the first resurrection. Blessed (happy, prosperous, to be admired) and holy is the person who takes part in the first resurrection; over these the second death [which is eternal separation from God, the lake of fire] has no power or authority, **but they will be priests of God and of Christ and they will reign with Him a thousand years.** Rev. 20:2b-6.*

That age is known as the Millennium where Christ himself will sit on the throne of David on earth, and He will rule and reign. Many will reign with Him and the earth will have her time of healing and rest. The whole earth will become like the garden in Eden, where Adam was created.

The body of Christ ought to preach the gospel of the kingdom to all the nations of the earth and to bring His kingdom and His will on earth as it is in heaven before Christ's return.

CHAPTER 2

THE GREAT COMMISSION

Jesus came up and said to them, "All authority (all power of absolute rule) in heaven and on earth has been given to Me. Go therefore and make disciples of all the nations [help the people to learn of Me, believe in Me, and obey My words], baptizing them in the name of the Father and of the Son and of the Holy Spirit, teaching them to observe everything that I have commanded you. Matt 28:18-20a.

Jesus summoned His twelve disciples and gave them authority and power over unclean spirits, to cast them out, and to heal every kind of disease and every kind of sickness... And as you go, preach, saying, 'The kingdom of heaven is at hand.' Heal the sick, raise the dead, cleanse the lepers, cast out demons. Freely you have received, freely give. Matt 10:1, 7-8.

Jesus walked among us not only to become our salvation but also as the example of how through Holy Spirit, we can operate here on the earth in Kingdom authority and power.

Because of Jesus suffering, death, resurrection and everything in between, the born again children of God now have the authority and power to fulfill the commission God gave Adam and Noah; the same commission Jesus left before He ascended in the cloud.

So God created man in His own image, in the image and likeness of God He created him; male and female He created them. And God blessed them [granting them certain authority] and said to them, "Be fruitful, multiply, and fill the earth, and subjugate it [putting it under your power]; and rule over (dominate) the fish of the sea, the birds of the air, and every living thing that moves upon the earth. Gen 1:27-28.

And the Lord God took the man (He had made), and settled him in the garden of Eden to cultivate and keep it. Gen 2:15.

*And God blessed **Noah** and his sons and said to them, "Be fruitful and multiply, and fill the earth"… As for you, be fruitful and multiply; Populate the earth abundantly and multiply in it." Gen 9:1, 7.*

Jesus came up and said to them, "All authority (all power of absolute rule) in heaven and on earth has been given to Me. Go therefore and make disciples of all the nations [help the people to learn of Me, believe in Me, and obey My words], baptizing them in the name of the Father and of the Son and of the Holy

THE GREAT COMMISSION

Spirit, teaching them to observe everything that I have commanded you. Matt 28:18-20a.

The Great Commission has not been fulfilled yet. It is clear in the Scriptures that God has not changed His mind about His people subduing, protecting and ruling over all the earth. Even though Adam conceded all his God given power and authority on the earth to the deceiver, the last Adam, Jesus, got them back transferring them to the born again children of God.

It is God's children's duty to disciple the whole earth in the things of God's kingdom. It is not about religious matters but about subduing all spheres of society and life under God's kingdom's ways. Everything has to function on the foundations of justice and righteousness. Jesus taught His disciples to pray "Your kingdom come, Your will be done, on earth as it is in heaven" Matt 6:10.

In heaven, everything is subject to God's ways. In heaven everything rejoices in the Lord always [delight, take pleasure in Him], the gentle *spirits* [their graciousness, unselfishness, mercy, tolerance, and patience] are known to all people. In heaven everything is true, honorable *and* worthy of respect, everything is right *and* confirmed by God's word, pure *and* wholesome, lovely *and* brings peace, everything is admirable *and* of good repute; there is excellence, everything is worthy of praise, just as well God's children on earth must *continually* think on these things [center their minds on them, and implant them in their hearts], and make them their way of life.

The body of Christ has to understand that when God created Adam and Eve in the garden of Eden, He chose to put the earth under man's authority and dominion. Psalm 115:16 says *The heavens are the heavens of the LORD,* **But the earth He has given to the children of men**. And Psalm 8:4-8 *What is man that You are mindful of him, And the son of [earthborn] man that You care for him? Yet You have made him a little lower than God, And You have crowned him with glory and honor.* **You made him to have dominion over the works of Your hands; You have put all things under his feet,** *All sheep and oxen, And also the beasts of the field, The birds of the air, and the fish of the sea, Whatever passes through the paths of the seas.*

The body of Christ has the misconception that the evil one still has the right over the earth because of Adam's disobedience; that was true until the second Adam, Jesus, took the keys of hell and death and triumphed over God's enemy. When He ascended to the Father and sprinkled His own perfect blood on the mercy seat, Jesus was given all power and all authority over all the power of the enemy and everything there is; then Jesus gave this power, authority and commission to the born again children of God.

The body of Christ has to be violent against the powers of darkness and take territory from the evil one, but it has to learn to subdue all systems of society, to protect them and to maintain/keep them. Nothing on earth should be subject or under the control of the evil one. The more the children of God become in the likeness of Jesus, the more difficult it will be for the evil one to maintain territory or to take it back. The time the evil one should be allowed to have on the earth are three and a half years, when "he who restrains the son of perdition will be taken out of the earth", the rest of the time should be in possession of God's children making earth as heaven is. Remember the restrainer are the Holy Spirit and the Bride of Christ which will be taken away at the rapture to go to the marriage of the Lamb in heaven.

Father God gave His Holy Spirit to His born again children to help them accomplish this task. Jesus broke the curse and gave His children authority and power to heal the earth and everything in it. "Occupy until I come" means to carry on the Father's business wherever the person's assignment is as God's delegate, messenger, sent forth with orders.

In the garden of Eden, Adam had everything available to him but he was responsible for subduing and protecting everything. He was expected to start in the garden of Eden, then little by little advance in territory until the whole earth became under the subjection and protection of the sons of God. Everything on earth was meant to look like and to function like the garden of Eden. Jesus was about His Father's business and so the Body of Christ ought to be.

In Luke 9:1-2 we read *Now Jesus called together the twelve [disciples] and gave them [the right to exercise] power and authority over all the demons and to heal diseases. Then He sent them out [on a brief journey] to preach the kingdom of God and to perform healing.*

Luke 10:1 says: *Now after this the Lord appointed seventy others, and* **sent them out ahead of Him**, *two by two,* **into every city and place where He was about to go**. The sent ones had specific instructions of what to do: **Whenever you go into a city** *and they welcome you, eat what is set before you; and* **heal those in it who are sick** *[authenticating your message]*, **and say to them, 'The kingdom of God has come near to you.'** *Luke 10:8-9.* Then Jesus states that some cities will not receive the message: *But whatever city you enter and they do not welcome you, go out into its streets and say, 'Even the dust of your city which clings to our feet we wipe off in protest against you [breaking all ties];* **yet understand this, that the kingdom of God has come near [and you rejected it].'** *Luke 10:10-11.*

Luke 24:47 *and that repentance [necessary] for forgiveness of sins would be preached in His name (Jesus) to all the nations, beginning from Jerusalem.*

The body of Christ must understand that God has given the command to go into every city of the world to heal the sick, cast out demons, raise the dead, cleanse the lepers (break the curses due to sin). Notice all these - sickness, demonic oppression and possession, death, and curses – are works of the evil one, which Jesus defeated through His sacrifice and resurrection. But also to preach the good news and to disciple or teach the nations of the world about the Kingdom of God and how to live on earth as it is in heaven. Many cities will receive and embrace God's messengers and the gospels, and will learn and operate in God's ways and principles; the reward and blessings of God will be in their midst, these will be called sheep cities and sheep nations. Unfortunately many other cities will reject the message and will even kill the messengers, giving themselves to sin and abominable things, but the time of God's wrath will come and they will be judged accordingly as goat cities and goat nations.

That's a pattern of God's way of taking over the nations to give them to Jesus as His inheritance. Jesus gave God's children the great commission, He sent them out ahead of Him to preach the gospel of salvation and of the kingdom of God and to disciple all the nations of the world (Matt 24;14) into every city and place where Jesus is about to go as the King of Kings and Lord of Lords. When Jesus returns, everybody must know who He is.

In like manner, God sent John the Baptist "to prepare the way of the Lord". John prepared the way for the time of Jesus public ministry. When John the Baptist appeared in the scene after years in the wilderness, he wasn't anything like the priests who ruled under the law of Moses. John smelled, dressed, ate and looked very different from the Pharisees and Sadducees, yet Jesus said in Luke 7:28 that up to that day there was not human greater than John the Baptist, but Jesus went ahead stating that yet he who is least in the kingdom of God (the born again believer) is greater [in privilege] than John the Baptist. Just like John the Baptist, our Lord's great commission is for God's children to prepare the way of the Lord for His second coming.

We read the same with Joshua as the people of Israel crossed the Jordan river. *I will drive them out before you **little by little, until you have increased and are strong enough to take possession of the land...** for I will hand over the residents of the land to you, and you shall drive them out before you. You shall not make a covenant with them or with their gods. **They** shall not live in your land, because they will make you sin against Me; for if you serve their gods, it is certain to be a trap for you [resulting in judgment]." Exodus 23:30-33.*

In this period of God's grace, Jesus gave God's children the command **to drive the evil one out** of the land, to dismantle everything the evil one has done to the land and its inhabitants and to fulfill the great commission. From the day of Jesus' resurrection **they** are the evil spirits behind all kinds of evil and disobedience to God.

In the times of Joshua, there was a time between taking the land and possessing the land. The Israelite armies went to war, took the land and made sure it remained in their possession. The workers, the women and the children remained behind in a safe place until it was safe for them to move in the newly acquired land. When it was time for them to move in, they had to work to keep what they had in order to multiply, to become prosperous and strong. Afterwards they had to establish life according to the law of Moses.

In military terms, when a nation overcomes or defeats another nation, the overcomers take control of the defeated nation. Their military and government officials set up all rules and regulations in all areas of society to operate like the victorious nation. Often times, the religious high places are destroyed and replaced by the religious buildings and rules of the overcomer nation's religious beliefs, or they take over the magnificent buildings to become places of worship of their own religion. The city streets planning, architecture, house decor, dress protocols, laws, currency and even language are changed. After all this is set in place, then the overcoming king comes to spend time in the newly acquired nation and with the people. It is not the king's job to do it him/herself. He/She shows up when everything is set in place and motion.

The Father is still waiting for the body of Christ to fulfill this commission in every sphere of society, in every corner of the earth. Some may think that it will be during the millennium, and it will be, but the commission to do it now has been consistent throughout all the history of mankind. And after all, the born of the Spirit children of God are the body of Christ on the earth, so Jesus is actually on earth right now, multiplied a gazillion times, empowered by the Spirit of the Living God.

Jesus said in Luke 9:57-62: (verse 60) *"Allow the [spiritually] dead to bury their own dead; but as for you, go and **spread the news about the kingdom of God**."* (verse 62) *"No one who puts his hand to the plow and looks back [to the things left behind] is fit **for the kingdom of God**."*

When the church understands and awakens to this truth, and decides to actually act as the hands, feet, mouth, etc of

Jesus with power and authority, then the time will be much closer to the taking away of the saints and the three and a half years will be given to the evil one. Then... a thousand years under the ruling of King Jesus!! Hallelujah!!

CHAPTER 3

THE BRIDE MAKES HERSELF READY

Let us rejoice and shout for joy! Let us give Him glory and honor, for the marriage of the Lamb has come [at last] and His bride (the redeemed) has prepared herself. She has been permitted to dress in fine linen, dazzling white and clean – for the fine linen signifies the righteous acts of the saints [the ethical conduct, personal integrity, moral courage, and godly character of believers]. Revelation 19:7, 8.

Another thing God is expecting the body of Christ to fulfill before the taking away of the saints, is the bride who has made herself ready to marry His Son. Too many born again believers, either don't know about the marriage of the Lamb, don't care about it, or they think that salvation is the only requirement to marry King Jesus.

In the spirit there's no male or female so the believers in Jesus Christ whether male or female can make themselves ready to become the bride of Christ. The marriage of the Lamb is a spiritual event.

In the book of Revelation chapter 19 verses 7 and 8 we clearly read that the bride (the redeemed) has prepared or made herself ready for the marriage. She is dressed in fine linen (the righteous acts of the saints) dazzling white and clean. It is talking about ethical conduct, personal integrity, moral courage, and godly character of believers. This is a call for a much higher standard in the life of a believer in Jesus Christ. The apostle Paul explains what the act of salvation does:

... just as Christ also loved the church and gave Himself up for her so that He might sanctify the church, having cleansed her by the washing of water with the word [of God], so that [in turn] He might present the church to Himself in glorious splendor, without spot or wrinkle or any such thing, but that she would be holy [set apart for God] and blameless. Eph. 5:25b-27.

When a person is born again in the spirit by believing in Jesus Christ, the blood of Jesus cleanses the person and erases all records of sin from the past. At the moment of being born again, that person is in the spirit, glorious to look at, perfect and without spot or wrinkle, BUT the apostle Paul states in his letters that the believer ought to change the lifestyle and the old worldly ways, to change all the old habits for new better ones to maintain the state of holiness as we read in Ephesians 5:1-25 and Galatians 5:19-21. It means to change our mind or to "renew our mind" by the washing of the word of God. Paul's letters have much to say about that. By changing our minds (mind/thoughts, will and emotions), we separate ourselves from the world and draw closer to God. We turn from having earthly viewpoints and experiences, to heavenly ones. Paul also teaches that we must subdue our bodies or to subject them to our spirits, because a born again spirit is now directly connected to the Holy Spirit. In some places in the Bible it's called "to crucify the flesh", which means to abstain from unholy, defiling desires of the body such as sexual immorality, impurity and sensuality (total irresponsibility, lack of self control), idolatry, sorcery, hostility, strife, jealousy, fits of anger, disputes, dissensions, factions [that promote heresies], envy, drunkenness, riotous behavior, conceited, challenging or provoking one another, envying one another, gluttony, etc.

Jesus says that the Holy Spirit will only speak what Father God says. Imagine the creator of the universe and everything there is, visible and invisible to the human eye, desires to communicate with you. The more the believer in Jesus Christ becomes separated for God, the clearer he/she will hear God, will draw closer to Him and will have revelation and understanding of God's treasures. As a whole, the believers make the church. The church is not the building where the believers gather together, the church *is* the believers.

The more the church allows the Holy Spirit to help her and to teach her, the more opportunity the church will have to become the bride of Christ and to get herself ready for the marriage of the Lamb.

John the Baptist talks about the bride, the bridegroom and the friends of the bridegroom:

He who has the bride is the bridegroom; but the friend of the bridegroom, who stands and listens to him, rejoices greatly because of the bridegroom's voice. So this pleasure and joy of mine is now complete. John 3:29.

John the Baptist is pretty much saying that he is a friend of the bridegroom, he had a job to do for his friend and then he got out of the way to allow the bridegroom do what He needed.

In the book of Ester we read how a virgin makes herself ready for a king.

… Hadassah, that is Esther… was beautiful of form and face… so it came about when the king's command and his decree were proclaimed and when many young women were gathered together in the citadel of Susa into the custody of Hegai, that Esther was taken to the king's palace [and placed] in the custody of Hegai, who was in charge of the women. Now the young woman pleased Hegai and found favor with him. So he quickly provided her with beauty preparations and her [portion of] food, and he gave her seven choice maids from the king's palace; then he transferred her and her maids to the best place in the harem. Now when it was each young woman's turn to go before King

THE BRIDE MAKES HERSELF READY

Ahasueros, after the end of her twelve months under the regulations for the women – for the days of their beautification were completed as follows; six months with oil and myrrh and six months with [sweet] spices and perfumes and the beauty preparations for women – then the young woman would go before the king in this way; anything that she wanted was given her to take with her from the harem into the king's palace... now as for Esther... when her turn came to go in to the king, she requested nothing except what Hegai... advised. And Esther found favor in the sight of all who saw her... Now the king loved Esther more than all the other women, and she found favor and kindness with him more than all the [other] virgins, so that he set the royal crown on her head and made her queen... Then the king held a great banquet, Esther's banquet, for all his officials and his servants; and he made a festival for the provinces and gave gifts in accordance with the resources of the king. Esther 2:8-18.

Esther was a beautiful of form and face virgin, but that was not enough to present her to the king. In like manner the born again believer, even though is clean and made righteous before the Lord, is not suit yet to marry the king. Let's remember the wise and the foolish virgins in Matthew 25:1-13, just because they were all virgins and they were all waiting for the bridegroom, doesn't mean they all entered to the wedding banquet, and the foolish ones were denied entrance because they were not ready.

Hebrews 9:27-28 says: *And just as it is appointed and destined for all men to die once and after this [comes certain] judgment,* *so Christ, having been offered once and once for all to bear [as a burden] the sins of many, will appear a second time [when he returns to earth], not to deal with sin, but to bring salvation **to those who are eagerly and confidently waiting for Him**.*

According to the regulations for the women destined for the king, they spent six months with oil and myrrh and six months with sweet spices and perfumes and the beauty preparations for women. It took one year for the beautiful virgin to be ready to see the king. She had to be of a sweet fragrance and soft to the touch. In like manner, the bride of Christ has to make herself ready to be of a sweet fragrance to the Lord. The apostle Paul wrote about the fragrance of the Lord, and the fragrance of the believer, like in 2 Corinthians 2:15-16 *for we are the sweet fragrance of Christ to [which ascends] to God.* In the Song of Solomon 4:10-14 we read about the bride's fragrance of the oils and of her garments. Sin makes a person stink in the spirit. The born again believer has to continually judge himself/herself to keep the sweet fragrance of the Lord. The Lord says "be holy for I am holy" (1 Peter 1:16). That means separate yourself from the world and get closer to God. The believer ought to abstain from obscenity, foolish talk or coarse joking, which are out of place (Gal 5:4), gossip or what some call "networking" is unacceptable (Romans 1:29). The more separated for God we become the sweeter the fragrance to the Lord. No stinky person will marry the king.

Esther found favor before Hegai who was in charge of the virgins in the harem so he quickly provided her with beauty preparations and her portion of food, and he gave her seven choice maids from the king's palace; then he transferred her and her maids to the best place in the harem. Then we read that she requested nothing except what Hegai advised to meet the king.

Hegai knew the best helpers, the best food, the best place, the best garments, the best behavior to please the king, and Esther heeded to his advice and did as Hegai and her maids taught her. The beauty preparations were one part of her learning but there was more that she needed to learn before she met the king. It was much more than one night with the king, she had to learn to please him in every way, she had to learn how to be a queen because that was possible from that one night with him.

This is why the apostle Paul wrote such instructions in his letters. He had a revelation of Jesus Christ, he met Jesus in the spirit, he met the king and was instructed what was needed for the church to become the bride. The Holy Spirit is the one that gives the believer revelation to understand that it is not an issue of religion or control but an issue of love towards the King of Majesty who deserves the best bride, one without spot or wrinkle, one dazzling and radiant with holiness and purity, righteous and sweet smelling. A bride who is so in love with her bridegroom that will do everything the Holy Spirit tells her to make herself ready to marry the King. He gave himself for her, to rescue her, to redeem her, He is absolutely worthy of a glorious bride.

Father God will not send Jesus to get His bride until she is gloriously ready.

CHAPTER 4

THE UNITY OF THE FAITH

I am no longer in the world; yet they are in the world, and I am coming to you. Holy Father, keep them in Your name, the name which You have given Me, so that they may be one just as We are...

I have given them the glory and honor which you have given Me, that they may be one, just as we are one. John 17:11, 22.

Make every effort to keep the oneness of the Spirit in the bond of peace [each individual working together to make the whole successful]... to build up the body of Christ [the church]; until we all reach oneness in the faith and in the knowledge of the Son of God [growing spiritually] to become a mature believer, reaching to the measure of the fullness of Christ [manifesting His spiritual completeness and exercising our spiritual gifts in unity]. So that we are no longer children [spiritually immature], tossed back and forth [like ships on a stormy sea] and carried about by every wind of [shifting] doctrine, by the cunning and trickery of [unscrupulous] men, by the deceitful scheming of people ready to do anything [for personal profit]. Eph. 4:3, 12b-14.

Jesus prayed to Father God that those who believed and would believe in Him would become one, just as Father God and Jesus are one [along with the Holy Spirit]. It is not likely that Jesus will come back without seeing first His prayer answered.

The apostle Paul not only encouraged the church to attain unity in the faith and the spirit but he gave the reason and the need for it: that the church will become spiritually mature.

As of 2022, the body of Christ is way too fragmented by doctrines and denominations that can't reach unity. Here, I'm talking about those who believe that Jesus Christ is the Son of the Living God, that the eternal God came down in the flesh, lived among men and was crucified and died for the sins of mankind, to restore communion between mankind and Christ's loving Heavenly Father, that Father God resurrected Jesus by the power of His Holy Spirit, ascended to heaven and is seated at the right hand of the Majesty of God. That Jesus Christ is The Door and The Only Way to Father God and the kingdom of heaven. These believers around the world make the body of Christ on the earth. These believers are called to be in the unity of the faith to become mature sons of God. This unity should be beyond religious doctrines and denominations. The evil one has done a good job dividing the body of Christ through religion. Religion is not of God, it was the **religious spirit** that killed Jesus, and throughout the history of mankind has persecuted, tortured and killed the servants of God, and the followers of Jesus.

The religious spirit's assignments are: to keep the body of Christ fragmented through doctrines and foolish arguments, to discredit every move of God and to quench the move of the Holy Spirit in a group of people. It will attribute the work of the Holy Spirit to the evil one like in Matthew 12:22-28 where the pharisees said it was only by the prince of demons, that Jesus drove out demons. At to what Jesus replied that a kingdom divided against itself will be ruined. I say a body of Christ divided against itself is ruined, lame and powerless.

Every time the Holy Spirit has moved among God's people, great divisions have transpired, and have exposed the groups under the rule of a religious spirit.

When John the Baptist was released to prepare the way of the Lord, he did things that had not been done in a long time if at all. He dressed like Elijah, one of the prophets of old – 2 Kings 1:8 NIV *They replied, "He was a man with a garment of hair and with a leather belt around his waist". The king said, "That was Elijah the Tishibite".* - Matt 3:4a NIV *John's clothes were made of camel's hair, and he had a leather belt around his waist.* - But the Bible has no record that John did any signs and miracles like Elijah, yet Jesus said: *"I tell you the truth: Among those born of women there has not risen anyone greater that John the Baptist; yet he who is least in the kingdom of heaven is greater than he"...* Read Matthew 11:11-14.

John's message was to Repent! for the kingdom of God is near, and then he baptized people in the river for the forgiveness of sins. The religious people of the day had followed the blood sacrifices of doves, sheep, goats and calves for the temporary remission of sins; the ordinances Israel received in the desert had become a profitable business for them, so when John the Baptist appeared they did not receive what God was doing: preparing the way and making the way straight for the revelation of their Savior, and the end of the blood sacrifices for the remission of sins. Now complete forgiveness of sins was becoming available. In Matthew 21:24-27 NIV we read that Jesus asked the pharisees a question: *"John's baptism -where did it come from? Was it from heaven, or from men? They discussed it among themselves and said, "If we say 'From heaven,' he will ask, 'Then why didn't you believe him?' But if we say, 'From men' – we are afraid of the people, for they all hold that John was a prophet." So they answered Jesus, "We don't know".* Their reputation and power over the people was more important than receiving what God was doing in their midst, hence they missed their day of visitation and killed the very One who was sent to redeem them.

The church has to be wise to accomplish the unity of the faith. There's a big difference to live in unity between the churches of the living God, and the unity that the world promotes with their logo COEXIST. The apostle Paul is clear in

2 Corinthians 6:14-18 *"Do not be yoked together with unbelievers. For what do righteousness and wickedness have in common? Or what fellowship can light have with darkness? What harmony is there between Christ and the evil one? What does a believer have in common with an unbeliever? What agreement is there between the temple of God and idols? For we are the temple of the living God. As God has said: "I will live with them and walk among them, and I will be their God, and they will be my people." Therefore come out from them and be separate, says the Lord. Touch no unclean thing, and I will receive you. I will be a Father to you, and you will be my sons and daughters, says the Lord Almighty."*

The church of the living God, the body of Christ, believes that the unaltered Holy Bible is the absolute Word of God and that it reveals God's nature, ways, and character. The body of Christ believes the Holy Spirit is sent by Father God to help, reveal, and empower it to accomplish/fulfill its destiny for which it was born of the Spirit of God. The body of Christ must not serve two masters and must not trust itself among unbelievers.

The body of Christ or the church's duty is to share with others the gospel of salvation and the gospel of God's kingdom, and to separate herself from any deceiving doctrine and deceiving belief to avoid confusion which in the end will make her sin against her God.

Being "a good person" will never be the way to heaven, Jesus Christ is the only way. The church has to love and have compassion on the unbelievers but must never mingle herself with them. Jesus says in Matthew 7:6 *Do not give dogs what is sacred; do not throw your pearls to pigs. If you do, they may trample them under their feet, and then turn and tear you to pieces."* People who are dead in their spirits, are under the control of the evil one, even when they are "very good people", without Christ, they have no strength to resist evil and they are going to hell. The evil one that owns them hates the born again believer so he will use the unbelievers to deceive the believers in Christ and to separate them from God, His Word and His ways. It may be a slow, almost unnoticeable process but it will end in rebellion and disobedience against the One who bought them with His own blood. No one is safe from this. Jesus says in Matthew 10:16 *Listen carefully: I am sending you out like sheep among wolves. Therefore be wise as serpents and as innocent as doves [have no self-serving agenda].*

The apostle Paul also encourages the church in Ephesians 5:1-21; here I emphasize verses 15 to 21. *Therefore see that you walk carefully [living life with honor, purpose, and courage; shunning those who tolerate and enable evil], not as the unwise, but as wise [sensible, intelligent, discerning people], making the very most of your time [on earth, recognizing and taking advantage of each opportunity and using it with wisdom and diligence], because the days are [filled with] evil. Therefore do not be foolish and thoughtless, but understand and firmly grasp what the will of the Lord is. Do not get drunk with wine, for that is wickedness (corruption, stupidity), but be filled with the [Holy] Spirit and constantly guided by Him. Speak to one another with psalms and hymns and spiritual songs, [offering praise by] singing and making melody with your heart to the Lord, always giving thanks to God the Father for all things, in the name of our Lord Jesus Christ, being subject to one another out of reverence for Christ.*

The Unity of the Faith in the body of Christ is of utmost importance as a testimony of Jesus Christ. Christians were reprimanded by the apostle Paul for the division there was in the local churches as we read in 1 Corinthians 1:10 *But I urge you, believers, by the name of our Lord Jesus Christ, that all of you be in full agreement in what you say, and that there be no divisions or factions among you, but that you be perfectly united in your way of thinking and in your judgment [about matters of the faith].*

In 1 Corinthians 12:14-27 Paul explains how the body of Christ should function:

For the [human] body does not consist of one part, but of many [limbs and organs]. If the foot says, "Because I am not a hand, I am not a part of the body," is it not on the contrary still a part of the body? If the ear says, "Because I am not an eye, I am not a part of the body," is it not on the contrary still a part of the body? If the whole body were an eye, where would the hearing be? If the whole [body] were an ear, where would the sense of smell be? But now [as things really are], God has placed and arranged the parts in the body, each one of them, just as He willed and saw fit [with the best balance of function]. If they all were a single organ, where would [the rest of] the body be? But now [as things really are] there are many parts [different limbs and organs], but a single body. The eye cannot say to the hand, "I have no need of you," nor again the head to the feet, "I have no need of you." But quite the contrary, the parts of the body that seem to be weaker are [absolutely] necessary; and as for those parts of the body which we consider less honorable, these we treat with greater honor; and our less presentable parts are treated with greater modesty, while our more presentable parts do not require it. But God has combined the [whole] body, giving greater honor to that part which lacks it, so that there would be no division or discord in the body [that is, lack of adaptation of the parts to each other], but that the parts may have the same concern for one another. And if one member suffers, all the parts share the suffering; if one member is honored, all rejoice with it.

Now you [collectively] are Christ's body, and individually [you are] members of it [each with his own special purpose and function].

The division among the followers of Jesus has caused great damage to the image of the body of Christ around the world. Believers and churches of Christ slander each other. "Christian" Ministries slander each other. Prophets slander each other. Churches don't work side by side to spread of the gospel of salvation and the gospel of the kingdom. You may say "we are very close and loving at our church family", that's very good, how does your church family relate to the body of Christ on the other side of town? That would be the next step in uniting the body of Christ. I am not saying they all have to become under the same name, the same pastor, the same church banner, the same denomination... As one body, Christ's body, it should be Jehova Nissi "the Lord is our banner". Make sure your relationship with the other organs of the body of Christ is just as good as it is with the other parts of the body in your church family.

The apostle Paul talks about it in 2 Timothy 2:14-17a. *Keep reminding them of these things. Warn them before God against quarreling about words; it is of no value, and only ruins those who listen. Do your best to present yourself to God as one approved, a workman who does not need to be ashamed and who correctly handles the word of truth. Avoid godless chatter, because those who indulge in it will become more and more ungodly. Their teaching will spread like gangrene.*

Some "Christians" have sided with the evil one, the accuser of the brethren and do his job. We read in Revelation 12 about the woman and the dragon and in verse 10b we read: *For the accuser of our brothers, who accuses them before our God day and night...* The "Christians" that accuse the brethren day and night are operating under the dragon spirit. Stay away from them, remember the true follower of Christ has to be occupied with Father God's business, representing our Loving Father well, spreading the gospels and being a good example of holiness, love, compassion and hope. Don't even listen to those who are slandering the brethren, don't replicate their behavior and don't share their garbage. The One who knows the hearts and the Truth is God, He will judge us all. 1 John 4:6 says *We [who teach God's word] are from God [energized by the Holy Spirit], and whoever knows God [through personal experience] listens to us [and has a deeper understanding of Him]. Whoever is not of God does not listen to us. By this we know [without any doubt] the spirit of truth [motivated by God] and the spirit of error [motivated by satan -noun not capitalized on purpose-].* According to the apostle John we ought to focus our attention and effort to the One who is Worthy of all the glory, honor, praise, authority, power, majesty, to the King of Kings and the Lord of Lords, the lamb of God, Jesus. We ought to strive to boldly enter before the throne of grace of our Father God and desire with all our hearts to know God and to have a relationship with Him, an experiential relationship, beyond head knowledge; and to follow the instructions of His Holy Spirit to be occupied in our Father's business. That's the only way to discern the spirit of error. It has to become personal and not by following others, no matter how mature we think they are or how much revelation we think they have. Remember Christians are supposed to be followers of Christ.

God is waiting for his sons and daughters to mature so He can trust them to rule His kingdom. Jesus and Paul said the same: "there's much more I want to share with you but you can't bare it". For instance in John 16:12; 1 Corinthians 3:1, 2; and, in Hebrews 5:11-14 we read *Concerning this we have much to say, and it is hard to explain, since you have become dull and sluggish in [your spiritual] hearing and disinclined to listen. For though by this time you ought to be teachers [because of the time you have had to learn these truths], you actually need someone to teach you again the elementary principles of God's word [from the beginning], and you have come to be continually in need of milk, not solid food. For everyone who lives on milk is [doctrinally inexperienced and] unskilled in the word of righteousness, since he is a spiritual infant. But solid food is for the [spiritually] mature, whose senses are trained by practice to distinguish what is morally good and what is evil.*

God needs mature sons and daughters to rule and reign with Christ. Our life on earth is our training camp. We have to end our race while we're here on the earth. The end of the kingdom age and the taking of His bride will not happen until the body of Christ operates in unity, becomes spiritually mature and learns to rule and reign in God's kingdom on earth. Romans 8:14 makes clear *For all who are allowing themselves to be led by the Spirit of God are sons of God.*, here the apostle is referring to mature sons. In the book of Revelation we read about the overcomers: Rev 2:26-28 *And he who overcomes [the world through believing that Jesus is the Son of God] and he who keeps My deeds [doing things that please Me] until the [very] end, TO HIM I WILL GIVE AUTHORITY and POWER OVER THE NATIONS; AND HE SHALL SHEPHERD and RULE THEM WITH A ROD OF IRON, AS THE EARTHEN POTS ARE BROKEN IN PIECES, as I also have received authority [and power to rule them] from My Father; and I will give him the Morning Star. He who has an ear, let him hear and heed what the Spirit says to the churches.'*

In Genesis 11:1-8 we read:

Now the whole earth spoke one language and used the same words (vocabulary). And as people journeyed eastward, they found a plain in the land of Shinar and they settled there. They said one to another, "Come, let us make bricks and fire them thoroughly [in a kiln, to harden and strengthen them]." So they used brick for stone [as building material], and they used tar (bitumen, asphalt) for mortar. They said, "Come, let us build a city for ourselves, and a tower whose top will reach into the heavens, and let us make a [famous] name for ourselves, so that we will not be scattered [into separate groups] and be dispersed over the surface of the entire earth [as the LORD instructed]." Now the LORD came down to see the city and the tower which the sons of men had built. And the LORD said, **"Behold, they are one [unified] people, and they all have the same language. This is only the beginning of what they will do [in rebellion against Me], and now no evil thing they imagine they can do will be impossible for them.** *Come, let Us (Father, Son, Holy Spirit) go down and there confuse and mix up their language, so that they will not understand one another's speech." So the LORD scattered them abroad from there over the surface of the entire earth; and they stopped building the city.*

Notice that anything that people in unity can imagine, they will accomplish. At Babel, their ultimate purpose was to overthrow God. They were in rebellion against God, so He came down and caused division through confusion and many different languages.

At Pentecost, after Jesus went back to heaven to sit at the right hand of the majesty of His Father God, that curse was reversed:

And when the day of Pentecost was fully come, they were all with one accord in one place. And suddenly there came a sound from heaven as of a rushing mighty wind, and it filled all the house where they were sitting. And there appeared unto them cloven tongues like as of fire, and it sat upon each of them. And they were all filled with the Holy Ghost, and began to speak with other tongues, as the Spirit gave them utterance. And there were dwelling at Jerusalem Jews, devout men, out of every nation under heaven. Now when this was noised abroad, the multitude came together, and were confounded, because that every man heard them speak in his own language. And they were all amazed and marvelled, saying one to another, Behold, are not all these which speak Galileans? And how hear we every man in our own tongue, wherein we were born? Acts 2:1-4 KJV.

Notice the 120 people in the upper room who were waiting for God The Father's gift were "in one accord", they were not only together but they were in unity. Through the Baptism of the Holy Spirit, God takes a hold of the believer's tongue and prays and declares the perfect will of God. The outward manifestation of the baptism of the Holy Spirit gives the body of Christ "one language" and because the believers don't understand what the Holy Spirit is saying, they can't oppose or contradict the perfect will of God. The prayer language of the believers have several purposes but their study does not pertain to this book.

The unity of the body of Christ creates a hedge of protection against the enemy, since the evil one goes around like a roaring lion seeking whom he may devour, the isolated christian is an easy prey.

This unity of the faith is not only among born again believers in Jesus Christ but it also talks about our unity with Messiah. When the christian is in unity or one with Jesus, then he/she is led of the Holy Spirit and that empowers the body of Christ to fulfill its purpose for which they were born. One can drive out a thousand but two can drive out ten thousand, this is exponential, and when in unity with Christ the gates of hell can not prevail against it.

The lack of unity in the church or the lack of discernment of the body of Christ is the reason why many Christians are weak, sick and die prematurely. This not only refers to the spiritual side of the body and the blood of Jesus as the sin offering but all the brethren carry the presence of God, they are God's children, ambassadors, carriers of His presence. They are the feet, hands, mouth, etc of Jesus. Anything done against God's children is done against God Himself, and it brings destruction.

When the apostle Paul explained how the body of Christ functions, he also showed how to treat the brethren at the stage they are at: even the weaker brethren are absolutely necessary, the brethren we consider less honorable should be treated with greater honor; the less presentable brethren should be treated with greater modesty; while the most presentable brethren do no require it. But God has combined the whole body, giving greater honor to those brethren which lack it, so that there would be no division or discord in the body that is, lack of adaptation of the parts to each other, but that the brethren may have the same concern for one another. And if one of the brethren suffers, all the church share the suffering; if one member is honored, all rejoice with him/her.

When the body of Christ understands the importance of being in one accord, in unity, bound with God's love, speaking God's language, having in mind only the agenda of God, they will operate in a coordinated effort and nothing will be impossible for them. This is God's desire: to have mature sons and daughters that work in unity truly believing that with Christ nothing is impossible. The group of believers that accomplishes this will be given the power that baby Christians can't handle. They will accomplish the will of God, they will completely fulfill the purpose for which they were born and finish their race in victory.

Father God will not send Jesus back until the Son of God gets His prayer answered. The ball is not in God's hands but in the church's hands.

CHAPTER 5

THEY WILL BE KNOWN FOR THEIR LOVE FOR EACH OTHER

By this everyone will know that you are My disciples, if you have love and unselfish concern for one another." John 13:35.

"This is My commandment, that you love and unselfishly seek the best for one another, just as I have loved you. John 15:12.

Does everyone know Christians for their love for each other? If not, this also has to be fulfilled before the end of the kingdom age and the taking away of the saints.

The apostles had to bring correction to the local churches which were struggling with certain issues. It seems like after 2000 years the church has not advanced much.

1 John 4:7-21 says: *Beloved, let us [unselfishly] love and seek the best for one another, for love is from God; and everyone who loves [others] is born of God and knows God [through personal experience]. The one who does not love has not become acquainted with God [does not and never did know Him], for God is love. [He is the originator of love, and it is an enduring attribute of His nature.] By this the love of God was displayed in us, in that God has sent His [One and] only begotten Son [the One who is truly unique, the only One of His kind] into the world so that we might live through Him. In this is love, not that we loved God, but that He loved us and sent His Son to be the propitiation [that is, the atoning sacrifice, and the satisfying offering] for our sins [fulfilling God's requirement for justice against sin and placating His wrath]. Beloved, if God so loved us [in this incredible way], we also ought to love one another.... But if we love one another [with unselfish concern], God abides in us, and His love [the love that is His essence abides in us and] is completed and perfected in us. By this we know [with confident assurance] that we abide in Him and He in us, because He has given to us His [Holy] Spirit. We [who were with Him in person] have seen and testify [as eye-witnesses] that the Father has sent the Son to be the Savior of the world.*

Whoever confesses and acknowledges that Jesus is the Son of God, God abides in him, and he in God. We have come to know [by personal observation and experience], and have believed [with deep, consistent faith] the love which God has for us. God is love, and the one who abides in love abides in God, and God abides continually in him. In this [union and fellowship with Him], *love is completed and perfected with us, so that we may have confidence in the day of judgment [with assurance and boldness to face Him]; **because as He is, so are we in this world**. There is no fear in love [dread does not exist]. But perfect (complete, full-grown) love drives out fear, because fear involves [the expectation of divine] punishment, so the one who is afraid [of God's judgment] is not perfected in love [has not grown into a sufficient understanding of God's love]. We love, because He first loved us. If anyone says, "I love God," and hates (works against) his [Christian] brother he is a liar; for the one who does not love his brother whom he has seen, cannot love God whom he has not seen. And this commandment we have from Him, that the one who loves God should also [unselfishly] love his brother and seek the best for him.*

As followers of Christ we must be transformed by love to respond in love. We have to read and to listen to the word of God to renew our minds so that our response to life will automatically be in love. Transforming one habit at a time, little by little we can give it to God and allow His Holy Spirit to intervene every time we need to be reminded of it.

In 1 John 4:8b we read that God **is** love. In 1 Corinthians 13:4-7 the apostle Paul gives us a description of the nature of God. Every time you read LOVE substitute it with GOD. Eventually substitute Love with your own name, that will help you recognize where you need Holy Spirit's grace to overcome that lack. If you need patience pray for more love, if you pray for patience you will get it through trials and tribulations (Rom 5:3). God's love is Agape Love, and it's the only kind that contains all the attributes of the nature of God.

Love endures with patience and serenity, love is kind and thoughtful, and is not jealous or envious; love does not brag and is not proud or arrogant. It is not rude; it is not self-seeking, it is not provoked [nor overly sensitive and easily angered]; it does not take into account a wrong endured. It does not rejoice at injustice, but rejoices with the truth [when right and truth prevail]. Love bears all things [regardless of what comes], believes all things [looking for the best in each one], hopes all things [remaining steadfast during difficult times], endures all things [without weakening]. 1 Cor. 13:4-7.

God also described Himself when He spoke to Moses on the mountain. God's name is the description of His attributes.

Then the LORD descended in the cloud and stood there with Moses as he proclaimed the Name of the LORD. Then the LORD passed by in front of him, and proclaimed, "The LORD, the LORD God, compassionate and gracious, slow to anger, and abounding in lovingkindness and truth (faithfulness); keeping mercy and lovingkindness for thousands, forgiving iniquity and transgression and sin; but He will by no means leave the guilty unpunished, visiting (avenging) the iniquity (sin, guilt) of the fathers upon the children and the grandchildren to the third and fourth generations [that is, calling the children to account for the sins of their fathers]." Exo. 34:5-7.

Paul tells us in Ephesians 5:1 *Therefore become imitators of God [copy Him and follow His example], as well-beloved children [imitate their father];* Every time we are tempted to respond differently than the nature of our heavenly Father, we can ask Holy Spirit "please give me grace to be like Jesus". It may take time because we have the habit to respond or to react a certain way but we can do all things through Christ who gives us strength (Phil 4:13) and we have the help of the same Spirit that raised Jesus from the dead (Rom 8:11) to help us overcome bad habits and to establish new good ones. When you read the Bible pay close attention to the verses that talk about this and meditate/think deeply about what they are saying. Ask Holy Spirit to help you understand what is being said and to help you to write them in your heart.

Remember our actions speak louder than our words. If every Christian strives to become love just like our Father God, Jesus and Holy Spirit, our domain will quickly become a nicer place.

Jesus is love, just like Father God. When he was on earth there were many who were so full of darkness that they despised Him. Please don't expect everyone around you to respond nicely to your new way of life. Demons may manifest around you to try to make you to respond according to your old ways. Do not give into it. Slowly but surely your consistent testimony of love will disarm those demons and will soften the hearts of those around you.

A famous missionary in Mozambique says: "Love looks like something" and "Stop for the One". In one way, Father God, who is Love, sent Jesus to purchase us back to Himself. Love looks like Jesus, His sacrifice really looked like something. It was and is much more than simply saying "I love you". At every opportunity, Jesus stopped for the One with compassion and love. It was Love that healed the sick, cast out demons, raised the dead, etc.

In James 2:15-16 the apostle teaches about faith expressed though works. *If a brother or sister is without [adequate] clothing and lacks [enough] food for each day, and one of you says to them, "Go in peace [with my blessing], [keep] warm and feed yourselves," but he does not give them the necessities for the body, what good does that do?* Love is the greatest of all three graces (1 Cor 13:13), and the works the apostle James is taking about ought to be fueled by love.

In the Old and New Testaments of the Bible, we find the consistent commandment of Love.

You shall love the LORD your God with all your heart and mind and with all your soul and with all your strength [your entire being]. Deuteronomy 6:5

Jesus answered, "The first and most important one is: 'HEAR, O ISRAEL, THE LORD OUR GOD IS ONE LORD; AND YOU SHALL LOVE THE LORD YOUR GOD WITH ALL YOUR HEART, AND WITH ALL YOUR SOUL (life), AND WITH ALL YOUR MIND (thought, understanding), AND WITH ALL YOUR STRENGTH.' This is the second: 'YOU SHALL [unselfishly] LOVE YOUR NEIGHBOR AS YOURSELF.' There is no other commandment greater than these." Mark 12:29-31.

Because God is love, and His desire is that we become like Him, the expression and our works of faith must represent Him at all times. What He expects from His children is simple and consistent.

"[Rather] is this not the fast which I choose, To undo the bonds of wickedness, To tear to pieces the ropes of the yoke, To let the oppressed go free And break apart every [enslaving] yoke? "Is it not to divide your bread with the hungry And bring the homeless poor into the house; When you see the naked, that you cover him, And not to hide yourself from [the needs of] your own flesh and blood? "Then your light will break out like the dawn, And your healing (restoration, new life) will quickly spring forth; Your righteousness will go before you [leading you to peace and prosperity], The glory of the LORD will be your rear guard. "Then you will call, and the LORD will answer; You will cry for help, and He will say, 'Here I am.' If you take away from your midst the yoke [of oppression], The finger pointed in scorn [toward the oppressed or the godly], and [every form of] wicked (sinful, unjust) speech, And if you offer yourself to [assist] the hungry And satisfy the need of the afflicted, Then your light will rise in darkness And your gloom will become like midday. "And the LORD will continually guide you, And satisfy your soul in scorched and dry places, And give strength to your bones; And you will be like a watered garden, And like a spring of water whose waters do not fail. "And your people will rebuild the ancient ruins; You will raise up and restore the age-old foundations [of buildings that have been laid waste]; You will be called Repairer of the Breach, Restorer of Streets with Dwellings. Isaiah 58:6-12.

He has told you, O man, what is good; And what does the LORD require of you Except to be just, and to love [and to diligently practice] kindness (compassion), And to walk humbly with your God [setting aside any overblown sense of importance or self-righteousness]? Micah 6:8.

In order to accomplish the will of God Jesus quoted the first part of Isaiah 61:1-8. In Luke 4:18-19 we read that He was the first one anointed to do that, but then He baptizes us with His Holy Spirit to do the whole job.

The Spirit of the Lord GOD is upon me, Because the LORD has anointed and commissioned me To bring good news to the humble and afflicted; He has sent me to bind up [the wounds of] the brokenhearted, To proclaim release [from confinement and condemnation] to the [physical and spiritual] captives And freedom to prisoners, To proclaim the favorable year of the LORD, <u>And the day of vengeance and retribution of our God, To comfort all who mourn, To grant to those who mourn in Zion the following: To give them a turban instead of dust [on their heads, a sign of mourning], The oil of joy instead of mourning, The garment [expressive] of praise instead of a disheartened spirit. So they will be called the trees of righteousness [strong and magnificent, distinguished for integrity, justice, and right standing with God], The planting of the LORD, that He may be glorified. Then they will rebuild the ancient ruins, They will raise up and restore the former desolations; And they will renew the ruined cities, The desolations (deserted settlements) of many generations. Strangers will stand and feed your flocks, And foreigners will be</u>

your farmers and your vinedressers. But you shall be called the priests of the LORD; People will speak of you as the ministers of our God. You will eat the wealth of nations, And you will boast of their riches. Instead of your [former] shame you will have a double portion; And instead of humiliation your people will shout for joy over their portion. Therefore in their land they will possess double [what they had forfeited]; Everlasting joy will be theirs. For I, the LORD, love justice; I hate robbery with a burnt offering. And I will faithfully reward them, And make an everlasting covenant with them. Isaiah 61:1-8.

The promises and rewards found in Isaiah 58 and 61, underlined above, have to happen before the second coming of Jesus. It is love, the goodness of God that leads people to repentance. If the world can't see God's amazing compassionate love in His church the world will not be drawn to Jesus.

Jesus commandments, like to love one another, have to be fulfilled by His body before Father God sends Him back to earth.

CHAPTER 6

THE JEWS WILL BE PROVOKED TO JEALOUSY

*So I say, have they (the Jews) stumbled so as to fall [to spiritual ruin]? Certainly not! But by their transgression [their rejection of the Messiah] salvation has come to the Gentiles, **to make Israel jealous** [when they realize what they have forfeited]. Now if Israel's transgression means riches for the world [at large] and their failure means riches for the Gentiles, how much more will their fulfillment and reinstatement be! But now I am speaking to you who are Gentiles. Inasmuch then as I am an apostle to the Gentiles, I magnify my ministry, **in the hope of somehow making my fellow countrymen jealous** [by stirring them up so that they will seek the truth] and perhaps save some of them…*

I do not want you, believers, to be unaware of this mystery [God's previously hidden plan]—so that you will not be wise in your own opinion—that a partial hardening has [temporarily] happened to Israel [to last] **until the full number of the Gentiles** has come in; and so [at that time] all Israel [that is, all Jews who have a personal faith in Jesus as Messiah] will be saved; just as it is written [in Scripture], Rom 11:11-14, 25-26.

This verses point at two things that have not happened yet: The Jews will be provoked to jealousy, and the full number of the Gentiles has to come in before the Jews come to Jesus in great numbers.

The purpose of having a nation of His own, called by His name, was to cover the earth with God's presence, displacing wickedness and the evil one. They had the same command Adam and Noah had. God made covenants with Noah, Abraham, Isaac, and later with Moses which covered a multitude of blessings best described in Deuteronomy 28:1-14:

"Now it shall be, if you diligently listen to and obey the voice of the LORD your God, being careful to do all of His commandments which I am commanding you today, the LORD your God will set you high above all the nations of the earth. All these blessings will come upon you and overtake you if you pay attention to the voice of the LORD your God.

You will be blessed in the city, and you will be blessed in the field. The offspring of your body and the produce of your ground and the offspring of your animals, the offspring of your herd and the young of your flock will be blessed. Your basket and your kneading bowl will be blessed. You will be blessed when you come in and you will be blessed when you go out.

*The LORD will cause the enemies who rise up against you to be defeated before you; they will come out against you one way, but flee before you seven ways. The LORD will command the blessing upon you in your storehouses and in all that you undertake, and He will bless you in the land which the LORD your God gives you. The LORD will establish you as a people holy [and set apart] to Himself, just as He has sworn to you, if you keep the commandments of the LORD your God and walk [that is, live your life each and every day] in His ways. **So all the peoples of the earth will see that you are called by the name of the LORD, and they will be afraid of you.** The LORD will give you great prosperity, in the offspring of your body and in the offspring of your livestock and the produce of your ground, in the land which the LORD swore to your fathers to give you. The LORD will open for you His good treasure house, the heavens, to give rain to your land in its season and to bless all the work of your hand; and you will lend to many nations, but you will not borrow. The LORD will make you the head (leader) and not the tail (follower); and you will be above only, and you will not be beneath, if you listen and pay attention to the commandments of the LORD your God, which I am commanding you today, to observe them carefully. Do not turn aside from any of the words which I am commanding you today, to the right or to the left, to follow and serve other gods.*

In the covenant with Moses and the people of Israel we see God's blessings in all areas of life. The blessings had a greater purpose than the well being of the Jews, it was that all the peoples of the earth would see that they were called by the name of the LORD, and they would be afraid of the people of God (the Jews).

When the Jews left Egypt after 400 years of slavery and hardship, they came out with the riches of the Egyptians, they lived in the desert for 40 years and they lacked nothing, their clothes and shoes didn't even wear out. They could have gotten into the promised land in less than a month but the Egyptian ways were so deep in their hearts that they rebelled against God and most of them died in the desert. For 40 years God gave them all the opportunity to speak to Him face to face, but just a few saw Him and only two (Moses and Joshua) embraced His presence. In Exodus 13:21 we read: *The [presence of the] LORD **was** going before them by day in a pillar (column) of cloud to lead them along the way, and in a pillar of fire by night to give them light.* God didn't send a cloud to keep them cool during the day and sent a pillar of fire to keep them warm at night, God WAS in the cloud and in the pillar of fire. His presence was with them at all times, but they didn't acknowledge Him. God toned down his powerful glory to where He could be in the midst of His people without destroying them. But only Moses said yes to God when He called him to meet face to face.

In Exodus 24:15-18 we read: *Then Moses went up to the mountain, and the cloud covered the mountain. The glory and brilliance of the LORD rested on Mount Sinai, and the cloud covered it for six days. On the seventh day God called to Moses from the midst of the cloud. In the sight of the Israelites the appearance of the glory and brilliance of the LORD was like consuming fire on the top of the mountain. Moses entered the midst of the cloud and went up the mountain; and he was on the mountain forty days and forty nights.*

Moses desire was to know God, to be deeply and intimately acquainted with God, recognizing and understanding His ways more clearly. Moses had the same desire God had had since He created Adam in the garden of Eden, the same desire of Enoch who walked so close to God that after 300 years of walking together He simply took him and Enoch was no more (Gen 5:24).

Moses said to the LORD, "See, You say to me, 'Bring up this people,' but You have not let me know whom You will send with me. Yet You have said, 'I know you by name, and you have also found favor in My sight.' Now therefore, I pray you, if I have found favor in Your sight, let me know Your ways so that I may know You [becoming more deeply and intimately acquainted with You, recognizing and understanding Your ways more clearly] and that I may find grace and favor in Your sight. And consider also, that this nation is Your people." And the LORD said, "My presence shall go with you, and I will give you rest [by bringing you and the people into the promised land]." And Moses said to Him, "If Your presence does not go [with me], do not lead us up from here. For how then can it be known that Your people and I have found favor in Your sight? Is it not by Your going with us, so

THE JEWS WILL BE PROVOKED TO JEALOUSY

that we are distinguished, Your people and I, from all the [other] people on the face of the earth?"

The LORD said to Moses, "I will also do this thing that you have asked; for you have found favor (lovingkindness, mercy) in My sight and I have known you [personally] by name." Then Moses said, "Please, show me Your glory!" And God said, "I will make all My goodness pass before you, and I will proclaim the Name of the LORD before you; for I will be gracious to whom I will be gracious, and will show compassion (lovingkindness) on whom I will show compassion." But He said, "You cannot see My face, for no man shall see Me and live!" Then the LORD said, "Behold, there is a place beside Me, and you shall stand there on the rock; and while My glory is passing by, I will put you in a cleft of the rock and protectively cover you with My hand until I have passed by. Then I will take away My hand and you shall see My back; but My face shall not be seen." Exodus 33:12-23.

So be ready by morning, and come up in the morning to Mount Sinai, and present yourself there to Me on the top of the mountain. No man is to come up with you, nor let any man be seen anywhere on the mountain; nor let flocks or herds feed in front of that mountain." Exo 34:2,3.

Then the LORD descended in the cloud and stood there with Moses as he proclaimed the Name of the LORD. Then the LORD passed by in front of him, and proclaimed, "The LORD, the LORD God, compassionate and gracious, slow to anger, and abounding in lovingkindness and truth (faithfulness); keeping mercy and lovingkindness for thousands, forgiving iniquity and transgression and sin; but He will by no means leave the guilty unpunished, visiting (avenging) the iniquity (sin, guilt) of the fathers upon the children and the grandchildren to the third and fourth generations [that is, calling the children to account for the sins of their fathers]." Moses bowed to the earth immediately and worshiped [the Lord]. And he said, "If now I have found favor and lovingkindness in Your sight, O Lord, let the Lord, please, go in our midst, though it is a stiff-necked (stubborn, rebellious) people, and pardon our iniquity and our sin, and take us as Your possession." Exo 34:5-9

Then God said, "Behold, I am going to make a covenant. Before all your people I will do wondrous works (miracles) such as have not been created or produced in all the earth nor among any of the nations; and all the people among whom you live shall see the working of the LORD, for it is a fearful and awesome thing that I am going to do with you. Exo 34:10.

Despite God's desire to do such things among His people, very few embraced Him and loved Him. Throughout Jewish history the majority of them have turned away from God. Their greatest opportunity of redemption became their worst curse, when they crucified their Savior and they declared *"Let [the responsibility for] His blood be on us and on our children!" Matt 27:25b.*

Such decision gave the Gentiles (the non Jews) the opportunity to draw near to God, and to become God's adopted sons and daughters. Paul's letter to the Romans chapter 11 explains it (read the whole chapter). And the gentiles got grafted into the family of Abraham by faith in the Lord Jesus Christ.

Christ purchased our freedom and redeemed us from the curse of the Law and its condemnation by becoming a curse for us—for it is written, "CURSED IS EVERYONE WHO HANGS [crucified] ON A TREE (cross)"— **in order that in Christ Jesus the blessing of Abraham might also come to the Gentiles,** *so that we would all receive [the realization of] the promise of the [Holy] Spirit through faith. Gal 3:13-14.*

When Jesus shared the bread and the wine representing His body and His blood, He spoke of a New Covenant.

And in the same way He took the cup after they had eaten, saying, "This cup, which is poured out for you, is the new covenant [ratified] in My blood. Luke 22:20.

The apostle Paul wrote in Hebrews 12:18-24 the contrast between a close relationship with God under the old covenant (like we saw with Moses) and the relationship between the born of the Spirit (through Christ Jesus) and Father God.

For you have not come [as did the Israelites in the wilderness] to a mountain that can be touched and to a blazing fire, and to gloom and darkness and a raging windstorm, and to the blast of a trumpet and a sound of words [such that] those who heard it begged that nothing more be said to them. For they could not bear the command, "IF EVEN A WILD ANIMAL TOUCHES THE MOUNTAIN, IT WILL BE STONED [to death]." In fact, so terrifying was the sight, that Moses said, "I AM FILLED WITH FEAR and trembling." **But you** *(the church of Christ) have come to Mount Zion and to the city of the living God, the heavenly Jerusalem, and to myriads of angels [in festive gathering], and to the general assembly and assembly of the firstborn who are registered [as citizens] in heaven, and to God, who is Judge of all, and to the spirits of the righteous (the redeemed in heaven) who have been made perfect [bringing them to their final glory], and to Jesus, the Mediator of a new covenant [uniting God and man], and to the sprinkled blood, which speaks [of mercy], a better and nobler and more gracious message than the blood of Abel [which cried out for vengeance].*

Now the born again, believer in Jesus Christ can: *Therefore let us [with privilege] approach the throne of grace [that is, the throne of God's gracious favor] with confidence and without fear, so that we may receive mercy [for our failures] and find [His amazing] grace to help in time of need [an appropriate blessing, coming just at the right moment]. Heb 4:16.*

The apostle Paul explains that the New Covenant, ratified in the blood of Christ, is much better.

For if that first covenant had been faultless, there would have been no occasion for a second one or an attempt to institute another one [the new covenant]. However, God finds fault with them [showing its inadequacy] when He says, "BEHOLD, THE DAYS WILL COME, SAYS THE LORD, WHEN I WILL MAKE and RATIFY A NEW COVENANT WITH THE HOUSE OF ISRAEL AND WITH THE HOUSE OF JUDAH; NOT LIKE THE COVENANT THAT I MADE WITH THEIR

FATHERS ON THE DAY WHEN I TOOK THEM BY THE HAND TO LEAD THEM OUT OF THE LAND OF EGYPT; FOR THEY DID NOT ABIDE IN MY COVENANT, AND SO I WITHDREW MY FAVOR and DISREGARDED THEM, SAYS THE LORD. "FOR THIS IS THE COVENANT THAT I WILL MAKE WITH THE HOUSE OF ISRAEL AFTER THOSE DAYS, SAYS THE LORD: I WILL IMPRINT MY LAWS UPON THEIR MINDS [even upon their innermost thoughts and understanding], AND ENGRAVE THEM UPON THEIR HEARTS [effecting their regeneration]. AND I WILL BE THEIR GOD, AND THEY SHALL BE MY PEOPLE. "AND IT WILL NOT BE [necessary] FOR EACH ONE TO TEACH HIS FELLOW CITIZEN, OR EACH ONE HIS BROTHER, SAYING, 'KNOW [by experience, have knowledge of] THE LORD,' FOR ALL WILL KNOW [Me by experience and have knowledge of] ME, FROM THE LEAST TO THE GREATEST OF THEM. "FOR I WILL BE MERCIFUL and GRACIOUS TOWARD THEIR WICKEDNESS, AND I WILL REMEMBER THEIR SINS NO MORE." When God speaks of "A new covenant," He makes the first one obsolete. And whatever is becoming obsolete (out of use, annulled) and growing old is ready to disappear. Hebrews 9:7-13.

The old covenant contained great blessings, wonders, miracles, fearful and awesome things.

We read in Proverbs 31:10-31 that women are also blessed with prosperity and authority, not authority over her husband but over everything else.

An excellent woman [one who is spiritual, capable, intelligent, and virtuous], who is he who can find her? Her value is more precious than jewels and her worth is far above rubies or pearls. The heart of her husband trusts in her [with secure confidence],

And he will have no lack of gain. She comforts, encourages, and does him only good and not evil All the days of her life. She looks for wool and flax And works with willing hands in delight. She is like the merchant ships [abounding with treasure]; She brings her [household's] food from far away. She rises also while it is still night And gives food to her household And assigns tasks to her maids. She considers a field before she buys or accepts it [expanding her business prudently]; With her profits she plants fruitful vines in her vineyard. She equips herself with strength [spiritual, mental, and physical fitness for her God-given task] And makes her arms strong. She sees that her gain is good; Her lamp does not go out, but it burns continually through the night [she is prepared for whatever lies ahead]. She stretches out her hands to the distaff, And her hands hold the spindle [as she spins wool into thread for clothing]. She opens and extends her hand to the poor, And she reaches out her filled hands to the needy. She does not fear the snow for her household, For all in her household are clothed in [expensive] scarlet [wool]. She makes for herself coverlets, cushions, and rugs of tapestry. Her clothing is linen, pure and fine, and purple [wool]. Her husband is known in the [city's] gates, When he sits among the elders of the land. She makes [fine] linen garments and sells them; And supplies sashes to the merchants. Strength and dignity are her clothing and her position is strong and secure; And she smiles at the future [knowing that she and her family are prepared]. She opens her mouth in [skillful and godly] wisdom, And the teaching of kindness is on her tongue [giving counsel and instruction]. She looks well to how things go in her household, And does not eat the bread of idleness. Her children rise up and call her blessed (happy, prosperous, to be admired); Her husband also, and

THE JEWS WILL BE PROVOKED TO JEALOUSY

he praises her, saying, "Many daughters have done nobly, and well [with the strength of character that is steadfast in goodness], But you excel them all." Charm and grace are deceptive, and [superficial] beauty is vain, But a woman who fears the LORD [reverently worshiping, obeying, serving, and trusting Him with awe-filled respect], she shall be praised. Give her of the product of her hands, And let her own works praise her in the gates [of the city].

The new covenant has better, greater promises but the greatest of all are:

* God's presence is not exclusively in an outward manifestation like a cloud or a pillar of fire, nor he sits in the arc of the covenant, in the Holly of Hollies inside the tabernacle of testimony, now God makes the born again believer His dwelling place. 1 Cor 3:16 *Do you not know and understand that you [the church] are the temple of God, and that the Spirit of God dwells [permanently] in you [collectively and individually]?* Our spirits lived inside God for eternity (He is the Father of lights, and He says we are light when we are born again), when He knitted our spirit in our flesh at conception, we were separated from God because of man's sinful nature, but at the born again experience, when our spirit is made alive again – reconnects with God -, God steps inside of us and we become His tabernacle.

* When we are born again our spirit is at the same time on earth hosting God and in heaven with Jesus: *And He raised us up together with Him [when we believed], and seated us with Him in the heavenly places, [because we are] in Christ Jesus,*

[and He did this] so that in the ages to come He might [clearly] show the immeasurable and unsurpassed riches of His grace in [His] kindness toward us in Christ Jesus [by providing for our redemption]. Eph 2:6,7 It is a mystery how God makes this happen.

* Father God sends the Holy Spirit to live inside of us if we ask Him. *In Him, you also, when you heard the word of truth, the good news of your salvation, and [as a result] believed in Him, were stamped with the seal of the promised Holy Spirit [the One promised by Christ] as owned and protected [by God]. The Spirit is the guarantee [the first installment, the pledge, a foretaste] of our inheritance until the redemption of God's own [purchased] possession [His believers], to the praise of His glory. Eph 1:13-14.* By God's Holy Spirit the born again believers can live in authority and the power of God.

The triune Almighty God chose to live inside those who believed and accepted His only begotten son Jesus.

The born again believers literally become new creatures never seen on earth before Christ's resurrection. Spiritual beings living in human flesh indwelled by God Himself.

Christians should not even look like spiritually dead mortal men. If the face of Moses shone after being in God's presence, shouldn't be a greater manifestation if we allowed God shine through us? God's manifest presence everywhere we go should provoke the Jews to jealousy.

The Jews Will Be Provoked To Jealousy

The many blessings of Abraham and his descendants should be overshadowed by God's children's blessings. After all, the Jews are His people but Christians are His sons and daughters. There should be no lack and no feeble among them. The least of their blessings should be at least those mentioned in Deuteronomy 28:1-14.

Until the born again believers in Christ Jesus learn, accept and manifest these truths, there's no reason for the Jews to be jealous. Poverty, sickness, and foolishness do not impress anyone and it misrepresents Father God who is absolutely good.

The Jews will be God's people forever, Gentile born again believers do not substitute the Jews.

The apostle Paul says in Romans 1:16 says: *I am not ashamed of the gospel, for it is the power of God for salvation [from His wrath and punishment] to everyone who believes [in Christ as Savior],* **to the Jew first** *and also to the Greek.*

And in Romans 3:22, 29-30

This righteousness of God comes through faith in Jesus Christ for all those [Jew or Gentile] who believe [and trust in Him and acknowledge Him as God's Son]. There is no distinction,… Or is God the God of Jews only? Is He not also the God of Gentiles [who were not given the Law]? Yes, of Gentiles also, since indeed it is one [and the same] God who will justify the circumcised by faith [which began with Abraham] and the uncircumcised through [their newly acquired] faith.

An in Ephesians 2:14-18

For He (Jesus) Himself is our peace and our bond of unity. He who made both groups—[Jews and Gentiles]—into one body and broke down the barrier, the dividing wall [of spiritual antagonism between us], by abolishing in His [own crucified] flesh the hostility caused by the Law with its commandments contained in ordinances [which He – Jesus - satisfied]; so that in Himself He might make the two into one new man, thereby establishing peace. And [that He] might reconcile them both [Jew and Gentile, united] in one body to God through the cross, thereby putting to death the hostility. AND HE CAME AND PREACHED THE GOOD NEWS OF PEACE TO YOU [Gentiles] WHO WERE FAR AWAY, AND PEACE TO THOSE [Jews] WHO WERE NEAR. For it is through Him that we both have a [direct] way of approach in one Spirit to the Father.

Keep in mind that Jesus Christ Himself was a Jew in the flesh as we can read in His genealogy in the gospels, even though many rejected Him, Jesus parents, the disciples and even the apostle Paul were Jews also and preached the gospel of salvation and of God's kingdom to both Jews and gentiles.

In Peter's first sermon on Pentecost, he explained "this" was "that":

but this is [the beginning of] what was spoken of through the prophet Joel: AND IT SHALL BE IN THE LAST DAYS,' says God, 'THAT I WILL POUR OUT MY SPIRIT UPON ALL MANKIND; AND YOUR SONS AND YOUR DAUGHTERS SHALL PROPHESY, AND YOUR YOUNG MEN

SHALL SEE *[divinely prompted]* VISIONS, AND YOUR OLD MEN SHALL DREAM *[divinely prompted]* DREAMS; EVEN ON MY BOND-SERVANTS, BOTH MEN AND WOMEN, I WILL IN THOSE DAYS POUR OUT MY SPIRIT *And they shall prophesy.* AND I WILL BRING ABOUT WONDERS IN THE SKY ABOVE AND SIGNS *(attesting miracles)* ON THE EARTH BELOW, BLOOD AND FIRE AND SMOKING VAPOR. 'THE SUN SHALL BE TURNED INTO DARKNESS AND THE MOON INTO BLOOD, BEFORE THE GREAT AND GLORIOUS DAY OF THE LORD COMES. 'AND IT SHALL BE THAT EVERYONE WHO CALLS UPON THE NAME OF THE LORD *[invoking, adoring, and worshiping the Lord Jesus]* SHALL BE SAVED *(rescued spiritually).'* Acts 2:17-21.

The outpouring of the Holy Spirit and fire at Pentecost was the beginning of the last days. The harvest was ready back then. We still are in the last days, we still are in harvest time, the wheat and the tares are mature and are recognizable, we should know who is wheat and who is tare. Good and evil mature together. Every generation has to go through judgment because by the third generation people don't know God and live as if there is no God so they don't fear Him. When God's judgments are on the earth the people learn righteousness: *The fear of the* LORD *is clean, enduring forever;* **The judgments of the** LORD **are true, they are righteous altogether**. *They are more desirable than gold, yes, than much fine gold; Sweeter also than honey and the drippings of the honeycomb. Moreover, by them Your servant is warned [reminded, illuminated, and instructed]; In keeping them there is great reward.* Psalm 19:9-11.

If we receive the purpose of the shaking, we receive the kingdom that can not be shaken and it will bring in the real new world order which is the kingdom of God on the earth through King Jesus. Jesus pointed at the harvest which was already ripe "back then". The harvest time started at Pentecost when 3,000 people were saved and baptized and received the Holy Spirit.

Then He [Jesus] said to His disciples, "The harvest is [indeed] plentiful, but the workers are few. So pray to the Lord of the harvest to send out workers into His harvest." Matt 9:37-38.

There still are billions of gentiles (and Jews) in the earth that need to hear the gospels. The number of gentiles means those who heard the gospel and accepted Jesus as their savior, this does not mean that some have been appointed to be saved and some to wrath, this means that the Gentiles, just like the Jews, will have the opportunity of salvation through hearing the good news and they will have the freedom to accept Jesus Christ as their savior or to reject Him. In 2 Peter 3:9b we read that Father God is *not wishing for any to perish but for **all** to come to repentance.*

Until the number of gentiles that will accept Jesus is fulfilled, the majority of Jews will keep the veil that stops them from seeing the truth about Jesus being their Messiah and accept Him as their true Savior, hence the end of the age and the coming of the Lord can not happen yet.

Remember that the evil one will only be given three and a half years of "reign", while King Jesus will have a thousand years to establish the kingdom of God on the earth.

CHAPTER 7

THE MANIFESTATION OF THE SONS OF GOD

For the earnest expectation of the creature waiteth for the manifestation of the sons of God
Rom 8:19 KJV

For [even the whole] creation [all nature] waits eagerly for the children of God to be revealed.
Rom 8:19 Amp.

The born again believers in Jesus Christ become children or sons of God by adoption.

But when [in God's plan] the proper time had fully come, God sent His Son, born of a woman, born under the [regulations of the] Law, so that He might redeem and liberate those who were under the Law, that we [who believe] might be adopted as sons [as God's children with all rights as fully grown members of a family]. And because you [really] are [His] sons, God has sent the Spirit of His Son into our hearts, crying out, "Abba! Father!" Therefore you are no longer a slave (bond-servant), but a son; and if a son, then also an heir through [the gracious act of] God [through Christ]. Gal 4:4-7.

Let's take a look at the manifestation of God's presence under the old covenant. God blessed richly and abundantly those who loved and feared Him. Sometimes it was out of His faithfulness to the covenant He made with Abraham, Isaac and Israel, but other times it was because of the obedience and reverence to God by His people.

* Enoch, did not experience death. There are records in the book of Enoch (one record included in the Bible) of the incredible works, revelation and prophecies he got from His very close relationship with the Lord. The Bible says about him:

By faith [that pleased God] Enoch was caught up and taken to heaven so that he would not have a glimpse of death; AND HE WAS NOT FOUND BECAUSE GOD HAD TAKEN HIM; for even before he was taken [to heaven], he received the testimony [still on record] that he had walked with God and pleased Him. But without faith it is impossible to [walk with God and] please Him, for whoever comes [near] to God must [necessarily] believe that God exists and that He rewards those who [earnestly and diligently] seek Him. Heb. 11:5,6.

THE MANIFESTATION OF THE SONS OF GOD

Jude 14-15 mentions Enoch's writings:

It was about these people that Enoch, in the seventh generation from Adam, prophesied, when he said, "Look, the Lord came with myriads of His holy ones to execute judgment upon all, and to convict all the ungodly of all the ungodly deeds they have done in an ungodly way, and of all the harsh and cruel things ungodly sinners have spoken against Him."

* Abraham was richly blessed by the Lord, and not only him but his nephew who was with him was blessed because of Abram's faith in God. When Abraham was one hundred years old, not only he begat the son of God's promise (Isaac) with his wife Sarah but later he also had several children with his concubines. God also promised him land and countless descendants. God revealed Abraham what He was about to do, and Abraham was able to argue with the Lord interceding for whole cities. God said Abraham was a prophet. Because of the Lord's blessings it didn't matter where he lived. He always prospered.

Now Abram was extremely rich in livestock and in silver and in gold. Gen 13:1.

...where he had first built an altar; and there Abram called on the name of the LORD [in prayer]. But Lot, who went with Abram, also had flocks and herds and tents. Now the land was not able to support them [that is, sustain all their grazing and water needs] while they lived near one another, for their possessions were too great for them to stay together. Gen. 13:4-6.

The LORD said to Abram, after Lot had left him, "Now lift up your eyes and look from the place where you are standing, northward and southward and eastward and westward; for all the land which you see I will give to you and to your descendants forever. I will make your descendants [as numerous] as the dust of the earth, so that if a man could count the [grains of] dust of the earth, then your descendants could also be counted. Gen. 13:14-16.

The LORD said, "Shall I keep secret from Abraham [My friend and servant] what I am going to do, since Abraham is destined to become a great and mighty nation, and all the nations of the earth will be blessed through him? For I have known (chosen, acknowledged) him [as My own], so that he may teach and command his children and [the sons of] his household after him to keep the way of the LORD by doing what is righteous and just, so that the LORD may bring upon Abraham what He has promised him."… As soon as He had finished speaking with Abraham the LORD departed, and Abraham returned to his own place. Gen 18:17-19, 33.

So from one man [Abraham], though he was physically as good as dead, there have sprung descendants whose number is as the stars of heaven and as countless as the innumerable sands on the seashore. Hebrews 11:12.

Now Abraham was old, [well] advanced in age; and the LORD had blessed Abraham in all things. Gen. 24:1.

Abraham took another wife, whose name was Keturah. She gave birth to Zimran, Jokshan, Medan, Midian, Ishbak, and

Shuah… All these were the sons of Keturah. Now Abraham gave everything that he had to Isaac; but to the sons of his concubines [Hagar and Keturah], Abraham gave gifts while he was still living and he sent them to the east country, away from Isaac his son [of promise]. The days of Abraham's life were a hundred and seventy-five years. Gen. 25:1-9.

* Sarah, Abraham's wife, conceived a child at her old age, and she was also very beautiful and youthful looking so that the King wanted her for himself.

By faith even Sarah herself received the ability to conceive [a child], even [when she was long] past the normal age for it, because she considered Him who had given her the promise to be reliable and true [to His word]. So from one man, though he was [physically] as good as dead, were born as many descendants AS THE STARS OF HEAVEN IN NUMBER, AND INNUMERABLE AS THE SAND ON THE SEASHORE. Hebrews 11:11, 12.

So Abimelech king of Gerar sent and took Sarah [into his harem]. Gen 20:2b.

* Isaac, just like his father Abraham, was very blessed of the Lord, and even in time of famine the land produced one hundred percent and his animals multiplied. The Lord richly blessed the work of his hands.

Now there was a famine in the land [of Canaan], besides the previous famine that had occurred in the days of Abraham. So Isaac went to Gerar, Gen 26:1.

Then Isaac planted [seed] in that land [as a farmer] and reaped in the same year a hundred times [as much as he had planted], **and the LORD blessed and favored him. And the man [Isaac] became great and gained more and more until he became very wealthy and extremely distinguished;** *he owned flocks and herds and a great household [with a number of servants], and the Philistines envied him. Now all the wells which his father's servants had dug in the days of Abraham his father, the Philistines stopped up by filling them with dirt. Then Abimelech said to Isaac, "Go away from here,* **because you are far too powerful for us."** *So Isaac left that region and camped in the Valley of Gerar, and settled there. Gen. 26:12-17.*

* Jacob was very prosperous and God blessed Laban because Jacob was with him. The goats and sheep gave birth as Jacob desired.

Jacob answered Laban, "You know how I have served you and how your possessions, your cattle and sheep and goats, have fared with me. For you had little before I came and it has increased and multiplied abundantly, and the LORD has favored you with blessings wherever I turned. Gen. 30:29-30.

So Jacob became exceedingly prosperous, and had large flocks [of sheep and goats], and female and male servants, and camels and donkeys. Gen. 30:43.

* Joseph, Abraham's great grandson, was blessed of the Lord. Even though he went through hardship he remained faithful to the Lord and ended up being second to Pharaoh, making

THE MANIFESTATION OF THE SONS OF GOD

Egypt the most powerful nation in the earth, and saving the people of Israel. Because the Lord was with Joseph, even the people around him was blessed.

Now Joseph had been taken down to Egypt; and Potiphar, an Egyptian officer of Pharaoh, the captain of the [royal] guard, bought him from the Ishmaelites, who had taken him down there. **The Lord was with Joseph, and he [even though a slave] became a successful and prosperous man**; *and he was in the house of his master, the Egyptian.* **Now his master saw that the Lord was with him and that the Lord caused all that he did to prosper (succeed) in his hand.** *So Joseph pleased Potiphar and found favor in his sight and he served him as his personal servant. He made Joseph overseer over his house, and he put all that he owned in Joseph's charge.* **It happened that from the time that he made Joseph overseer in his house and [put him in charge] over all that he owned, that the Lord blessed the Egyptian's house because of Joseph**; *so the Lord's blessing was on everything that Potiphar owned, in the house and in the field. So Potiphar left all that he owned in Joseph's charge; Genesis 39:1-6.*

So Pharaoh said to his servants, "Can we find a man like this [a man equal to Joseph], in whom is the divine spirit [of God]?" Then Pharaoh said to Joseph, "Since [your] God has shown you all this, **there is no one as discerning and clear-headed and wise as you are. You shall have charge over my house, and all my people shall be governed according to your word and pay respect [to you with reverence, submission, and** *obedience]; only in [matters of] the throne will I be greater than you [in Egypt]."* Then Pharaoh said to Joseph, "See, I have set you [in charge] over all the land of Egypt." **Then Pharaoh took off his signet ring from his hand and put it on Joseph's hand, and dressed him in [official] vestments of fine linen and put a gold chain around his neck. He had him ride in his second chariot; and runners proclaimed before him, "[Attention,] bow the knee!" And he set him over all the land of Egypt.** *Moreover, Pharaoh said to Joseph, "Though I am Pharaoh, yet without your permission shall no man raise his hand [to do anything] or set his foot [to go anywhere] in all the land of Egypt [all classes of people shall submit to your authority]." Then Pharaoh named Joseph Zaphenath-paneah; and he gave him Asenath, the daughter of Potiphera, priest of On (Heliopolis in Egypt), as his wife. And Joseph went out over all the land of Egypt [to inspect and govern it]. Gen. 41:38-45.*

* Moses was not only kept from being killed but he was raised and educated in the house of Pharaoh as his grandson. Moses was a friend of God, spoke to God face to face, and God gave him knowledge and wisdom to lead the whole nation of Israel. God also revealed to Moses the origins of creation of the universe and the earth, about Adam and Eve, and showed him the throne room in heaven.

It was at this [critical] time that Moses was born; and he was lovely in the sight of God, and for three months he was nourished in his father's house. Then when he was set outside [to die], Pharaoh's daughter rescued him and claimed him for herself, and cared for him as her own son. So Moses was educated in all the wisdom and culture of the Egyptians, and he was a man of power in words and deeds. Acts 7:20-22.

And see to it that you copy [exactly] their pattern (of the tabernacle) which was shown you on the mountain. Exo 25:40.

The Lord came down in a pillar of cloud, and stood at the Tent door and called Aaron and Miriam, and they came forward. And He said, Hear now My words: If there is a prophet among you, I the Lord make Myself known to him in a vision and speak to him in a dream. But not so with My servant Moses; he is entrusted and faithful in all My house. With him I speak mouth to mouth [directly], clearly and not in dark speeches; and he beholds the form of the Lord. Numbers12:5-8.

* Joshua prayed and the sun stood still. Many miracles happened during Joshua's time like the falling of the walls of Jericho.

Then Joshua spoke to the Lord on the day when the Lord gave the Amorites over to the Israelites, and he said in the sight of Israel, Sun, be silent and stand still at Gibeon, and you, moon, in the Valley of Ajalon! And the sun stood still, and the moon stayed, until the nation took vengeance upon their enemies. Is not this written in the Book of Jasher? So the sun stood still in the midst of the heavens and did not hasten to go down for about a whole day. There was no day like it before or since, when the Lord heeded the voice of a man. For the Lord fought for Israel. Josh 10:12-14.

In Hebrews 11 we read the amazing examples of the works the Lord did for and through His people.

Verses 23 to 34: *By faith (simple trust and confidence in God) he (Moses) instituted and carried out the Passover and the sprinkling of the blood [on the doorposts], so that the destroyer of the firstborn (the angel) might not touch those [of the children of Israel].*

[Urged on] by faith the people crossed the Red Sea as [though] on dry land, but when the Egyptians tried to do the same thing they were swallowed up [by the sea].

Because of faith the walls of Jericho fell down after they had been encompassed for seven days [by the Israelites].

[Prompted] by faith Rahab the prostitute was not destroyed along with those who refused to believe and obey, because she had received the spies in peace [without enmity].

And what shall I say further? For time would fail me to tell of Gideon, Barak, Samson, Jephthah, of David and Samuel and the prophets,

Who by [the help of] faith subdued kingdoms, administered justice, obtained promised blessings, closed the mouths of lions, Extinguished the power of raging fire, escaped the devourings of the sword, out of frailty and weakness won strength and became stalwart, even mighty and resistless in battle, routing alien hosts.

THE MANIFESTATION OF THE SONS OF GOD

Under the old lesser covenant we find that God blessed His people in amazing ways. The earth, the sun, the moon, the animals, angels, everything was moved in miraculous ways on behalf of God's people. This favor was given to only a few, because only a few purposed in their hearts to seek God, to have faith in Him, to trust Him, to love Him with all their hearts, souls and strength. The anointing was poured out in only a few, and it could be taken away.

The manifestation of His power and glory, mercy and virtues have the purpose of causing the nations to fear the Lord. The fear of the Lord is the beginning of wisdom, and that is the ultimate purpose of God, to bless the people, to cause them to live the fullness of life, to be personally loved by their maker and redeemer, their Father if they want Him. To turn the earth to look like the garden of Eden, blessed and at peace.

Nations feared Israel and the God of Israel. The closer they were to God the greater the manifestation of God's goodness. Every time the nation of Israel despised God and became rebellious and idolatrous His faithful ones were persecuted and killed, but they died as seeds producing many more like them, lovers and servants of the Most High God manifesting God's power on the earth.

All the wonders and miracles that God performed under the old covenant were always conditional. God's people seeked His face, prayed, interceded and asked Him, then God gave them instructions on how to go about it. Sometimes He did what people requested, sometimes He told them exactly what to do but the people had to follow His instructions exactly the way God said. Every time they disobeyed, they got in trouble and the nation of Israel suffered. Sin is the sting of death. In the old testament we don't see the same instruction happen twice, every time it was different, it made the people seek God's wisdom and knowledge for every new challenge. In Egypt Joseph was instructed to store food for seven years, but 400 years later, in the desert with Moses, God fed them Manna.

We read in King David's Psalm 8:

*Lord, our Lord, how excellent is your name in all the earth! You set your glory above the heavens! Out of the mouths of infants and nursing babies you have established strength on account of your adversaries, **in order to silence the enemy and vengeful foe.***

When I look at the heavens, the work of your fingers, the moon and the stars that you established— what is man that you take notice of him, or the son of man that you pay attention to him? You made him a little less than divine, but you crowned him with glory and honor. You gave him dominion over the work of your hands, you put all things under his feet: Sheep and cattle— all of them, wild creatures of the field, birds in the sky, fish in the sea— whatever moves through the currents of the oceans.

Lord, our Lord, how excellent is your name in all the earth!

The Manifestation of the Sons of God

Under the new covenant in Jesus blood, we have a better covenant, ALL the born again in Christ children of God have been given all the power and authority over all the power of the evil one and over the work of God's hands on earth. The anointing of His Holy Spirit is now available to all who want Him, and who would be so foolish to not desire Him!

If you then, evil as you are, know how to give good gifts [gifts that are to their advantage] to your children, how much more will your heavenly Father give the Holy Spirit to those who ask and continue to ask Him! Luke 11:13.

The Holy Spirit is given to the church to teach her, to give her revelation and knowledge of who God is, to understand His heavenly kingdom and God's own ways. To help her to get a hold of the complete purpose of the Word becoming flesh [Jesus], and everything the apostle Paul wrote in his letters to the believers. To encourage the church to live by faith so that she will become the manifested children of the Most High God.

The believer must seek God's face, pray, intercede, and ask Holy Spirit what to do in every specific situation. Sometimes He will say "shut up", sometimes "speak"; sometimes don't worry about what you will eat or wear, sometimes *"Go to the ant, oh lazy one, observe her ways and be wise, Which, having no chief, overseer or ruler, she prepares her food in the summer and brings in her provisions [of food for the winter] in the harvest."* Prov 6:6-8. The church has to be led by the Holy Spirit continually.

In Proverbs 26 verses 4 and 5 seem to contradict each other but it just means that we need the Holy Spirit to know what to do in a specific situation.

Do not answer [nor pretend to agree with the frivolous comments of] a [closed-minded] fool according to his folly, Otherwise you, even you, will be like him.

Answer [and correct the erroneous concepts of] a fool according to his folly, Otherwise he will be wise in his own eyes [if he thinks you agree with him].

In the Old Testament we see that every time God was present, God's glory was manifest. How much more the children of God, bought by the blood of His son Jesus, should manifest the presence of God in them with signs, wonders and miracles. A life lived as a new creature in Christ, transformed by the washing of God's word, totally abandoned to the leading of the Holy Spirit, in perfect communion with God will bring the manifestation of the sons of God that the creation is waiting for.

The body of Christ should dictate what happens in times of war, famine, weather disasters, etc instead of crying out for help and resources from the world. God put the body of Christ on the earth to be a solution to the world's problems, to be the head and not the tail, to rule and reign. That is the practical purpose of God living inside the believers in Christ, that Christ may manifest Father God's goodness by the power of Holy Spirit to the entire earth through His sons and daughters.

Only those who truly live connected to the vine (Jesus), and are constantly led of the Holy Spirit, being washed and transformed by the Word of God will allow God freedom to do whatever He wants through them. Without relationship there's no manifestation. The children of the Most High God must desire a relationship with their Heavenly Father, Jesus and Holy Spirit. This desire must be out of love, adoration and awe to know Him for who He is and not for what He provides. The blessings are a bonus of His goodness but nothing in the universe compares to being in the presence of perfect Love and perfect acceptance.

The second coming of Jesus will not happen until this is fulfilled. There is no way that what God did for and through His people in times past, will not happen now for and through His children under a better covenant.

CHAPTER 8

THE GREATER WORKS

*I assure you and most solemnly say to you, anyone who believes in Me [as Savior] will also do the things that I do; and he will do even greater things than these [in extent and outreach], because I am going to the Father. And I will do whatever you ask in My name [as My representative], this I will do, so that the Father may be glorified and celebrated in the Son. If you ask Me anything in My name [as My representative], I will do it. **"If you [really] love Me, you will keep and obey My commandments"**. John 14:12-15.*

Jesus is THE example for us to follow, He said If you really love me you will keep and obey My commandments. Jesus Himself lived a life of obedience to God as we read in Philippians 2:8-11

*After He (Jesus) was found in [terms of His] outward appearance as a man [for a divinely-appointed time], **He humbled***

Himself [still further] by becoming obedient [to the Father] to the point of death, even death on a cross. For this reason also [because He obeyed and so completely humbled Himself], God has highly exalted Him and bestowed on Him the name which is above every name, so that at the name of Jesus EVERY KNEE SHALL BOW [in submission], of those who are in heaven and on earth and under the earth, and that every tongue will confess and openly acknowledge that Jesus Christ is Lord (sovereign God), to the glory of God the Father.

God Almighty performed all kinds of signs and wonders through Jesus. Even though Jesus was and is forever God, He operated on earth as fully human subjected to the law and to the power of God by the Holy Spirit *"Men of Israel, listen to these words: Jesus of Nazareth, a Man accredited and pointed out and attested to you by God **with [the power to perform] miracles and wonders and signs which God worked through Him** in your [very] midst, just as you yourselves know— Acts 2:22.*

The Bible mentions just a few of the many signs, wonders and works that Jesus did:

And there are also many other things which Jesus did, which if they were recorded] one by one, I suppose that even the world itself could not contain the books that would be written. John 21:25.

Here's a brief list of some of the things Jesus did:

* Multiplied food	John 6:1-14; Matt 15:32-38
* Healed the man born blind	John 9:1-7
* Healed a demon possessed man	Luke 8:26-33
* Raised a dead girl and healed a sick woman	Luke 8:43-48
* Raised the dead	Luke 8:49-56; John 11:17-44
* Walked on water	Matt 14:22-33; John 6:16-21
* Was miraculously transported	John 6:21
* Rebuked the wind and stilled the sea	Mark 4:35-41
* Healed an ear cut off	Luke 22:50-51
* His anointing healed a woman	Luke 8:43-48
* Walked invisible through the crowd	Luke 4:28-30
* Healed a leper and a paralytic	Luke 5:12-26
* Turned water into wine	John 2:1-11

* Produced a large catch of fish	Luke 5:1-9: John 21:4-8
* Jesus was transfigured with God's glory	Matt 17:1, 2
* Interacted with the cloud of witnesses (talked to Moses and Elijah)	Matt 17:3
* Knew people's thoughts	Matt 12:25
* Saw Father God	John 5:19-20
* Heard Father God	John 12:49-50
* Drove out an evil spirit	Mar 1:21-26
* Knew people's thoughts	Luke 6:8
* Healed a man with a withered hand	Luke 6:6-10
* Knew the past and the future	Matt 24:1-46
* His anointing healed and delivered	Luke 6:17-19
* He had supernatural knowledge	John 4:29 (read verses from 7 to 30)
* He preached the gospel of the kingdom	Matt 4:23; Mark 1:35-39
* He is exactly like Father God	John 14:7-15

* Didn't have to be present to heal	Matt 8:5-13; John 4:46-54
* Jesus was ministered by angels	Matt 4:11
* He cursed a tree and it withered	Mark 11:11-14, 20-21
* He said we can move mountains	Mark 11:22-26

Jesus did all of these as the son of man. Even though He was God he did not operate as God on the earth. Part of Jesus mission was to become an example of what a person can do when he/she is completely submitted to Father God and His Holy Spirit. His ministry started after He was infilled by Holy Spirit (Luke 3:22). John the Baptist said Jesus will baptize with Holy Spirit and fire (Luke 3:16). Jesus spoke about Holy Spirit (John 14:16-29), and then He commanded His disciples and followers to wait for the Holy Spirit who was sent on the day of the Feast of Pentecost (Acts 2:1-4). 120 disciples and followers of Jesus, and later Paul, Jews and Gentiles, were baptized in the Holy Spirit with the outward sign of speaking in tongues, as we clearly read throughout the book of Acts.

Jesus' disciples (the twelve plus seventy more) had operated in some miracles of healing and deliverance in the name of Jesus when He sent them out:

[Whenever you go into a city and they welcome you, eat what is set before you; and heal those in it who are sick [authenticating

your message], and say to them, 'The kingdom of God has come near to you.'... The seventy returned with joy, saying, "Lord, even the demons are subject to us in Your name." Luke 10:8-9, 17.

And Jesus called the twelve [disciples] and began to send them out [as His special messengers] two by two, and gave them authority and power over the unclean spirits... So they went out and preached that men should repent [that is, think differently, recognize sin, turn away from it, and live changed lives]. And they were casting out many demons and were anointing with oil many who were sick, and healing them. Mark 6:7, 12-13.

But when the 120 people waiting at Pentecost were baptized in Holy Spirit and fire, they were brought into the deeper things of God as Jesus had promised:

And I will ask the Father, and He will give you another Helper (Comforter, Advocate, Intercessor—Counselor, Strengthener, Standby), to be with you forever— the Spirit of Truth, whom the world cannot receive [and take to its heart] because it does not see Him or know Him, but you know Him because He (the Holy Spirit) remains with you continually and will be in you.

"I will not leave you as orphans [comfortless, bereaved, and helpless]; I will come [back] to you. After a little while the world will no longer see Me, but you will see Me; because I live, you will live also. On that day [when that time comes] you will know for yourselves that I am in My Father, and you are in Me, and I am in you. The person who has My commandments and keeps them is the one who [really] loves Me; and whoever [really] loves

Me will be loved by My Father, and I will love him and reveal Myself to him [I will make Myself real to him]." Judas (not Iscariot) asked Him, "Lord, what has happened that You are going to reveal Yourself to us and not to the world?" Jesus answered, "If anyone [really] loves Me, he will keep My word (teaching); and My Father will love him, and We will come to him and make Our dwelling place with him. One who does not [really] love Me does not keep My words. And the word (teaching) which you hear is not Mine, but is the Father's who sent Me.

"I have told you these things while I am still with you. But the Helper (Comforter, Advocate, Intercessor—Counselor, Strengthener, Standby), the Holy Spirit, whom the Father will send in My name [in My place, to represent Me and act on My behalf], He will teach you all things. And He will help you remember everything that I have told you. Peace I leave with you; My [perfect] peace I give to you; not as the world gives do I give to you. Do not let your heart be troubled, nor let it be afraid. [Let My perfect peace calm you in every circumstance and give you courage and strength for every challenge.] You heard Me tell you, 'I am going away, and I am coming back to you.' If you [really] loved Me, you would have rejoiced, because I am going [back] to the Father, for the Father is greater than I. I have told you now before it happens, so that when it does take place, you may believe and have faith [in Me]. John 14:16-29.

And they were catapulted into greater works.

* There was the sound of a windstorm, and spiritual flames of fire came upon them when the Holy Spirit was sent to the 120 people in the upper room — Acts 2:1-3

* Supernaturally they spoke languages that were unknown to them and declared the great deeds of God. — Acts 2:4

* One anointed sermon convicted the hearts of about three thousand people who were born again and were baptized — Acts 2:40-41

* Peter heals a beggar who was crippled from birth — Acts 3:1-8

* The apostles did not miss a chance to boldly proclaim the good news — Acts 3:11-26

* Believers in Jesus fell dead after lying to the Holy Spirit — Acts 5:10

* Peter's shadow (anointing) healed all who were sick and those tormented by evil spirits when he passed by. — Acts 5:12-16

* People saw the apostles had been with Jesus — Acts 4:12-13

* They were full of the Holy Spirit and wisdom — Acts 6:1-7

* Even when they were persecuted and scattered, the apostles and disciples preached the word wherever they went	Acts 8:4
* Miracles and wonders happened when the gospel was preached	Acts 8:4-8
* They had supernatural knowledge	Acts 8:20-23
* Angels of the Lord spoke to them	Acts 8:26; Acts 27:23-24
* They were led by Holy Spirit	Acts 8:29; Acts 16:6-10
* Philip was miraculously transported by the Holy Spirit	Acts 8:39
* Disciples saw and/or heard Jesus in visions	Acts 9:10-15
* Jesus sometimes appears to the ones He calls	Acts 9:17-19, 27; Acts 22:14, 18, 21; Acts 23:11
* Holy Spirit gives boldness to preach the gospel of salvation and of the kingdom	Acts 9:27
* God speaks through visions	Acts 10:9-17; Acts 16:9
* All believers can receive the baptism of the Holy Spirit	Acts 11:15-17

THE GREATER WORKS

* There's visible angelic help	Acts 12:6-11
* Paul, led by the Holy Spirit cursed a sorcerer and false prophet	Acts 13:6-12
* Paul healed a man crippled from birth	Acts 14:8-10
* They had supernatural discernment of spirits	Acts 16:16-18
* They were supernaturally freed	Acts 16:25-26
* God's anointing remained in Paul's handkerchiefs and aprons that healed and delivered those who touched them	Acts 19:11-12
* They raised the dead	Acts 20:9-12
* Women also prophesy	Acts 21:9
* Didn't die from venomous snake	Acts 28:1-6. Jesus gave authority Luke 10:19
* Saw heaven	2 Cor 12:1-4; Rev 4:1-11
* Paul was taught by Jesus Himself	Gal 1:11-12

It's worth to notice that if it's found in the Bible it's a miracle or a wonder, if it's not found in the Bible, it's a greater miracle. Christians ought to allow God to do what He wants and not to limit Him with unbelief. Some people quote

Matthew 24:24 to justify their unbelief: *"For false Christs and false prophets will appear and they will provide great signs and wonders, so as to deceive, if possible, even the elect (God's chosen ones)."*

To know when it's God's true miracle and/or wonder we have to pay attention to the message and not to the sign itself. Jesus rebuked the Pharisees and Sadducees for demanding signs: *An evil and [morally] unfaithful generation craves a [miraculous] sign. Matt 16:4.*

And Jesus remarked that the people in Samaria believed in Him because of His Word: *Many more believed in Him [with a deep, abiding trust]* **because of His word** *[His personal message to them]; and they told the woman, "We no longer believe just because of what you said; for [now] we have heard Him for ourselves and know [with confident assurance] that this One is truly the Savior of [all] the world." John 4:41-42.*

But in Galilee, even with the signs, they didn't believe He was their Messiah: *Then Jesus said to him, "Unless you [people] see [miraculous] signs and wonders, you [simply] will not believe." John 4:48.*

The body of Christ has to desire the message, the good news of salvation, the gospel of the kingdom, the treasures of Jesus' inheritance. The miracles and wonders are to validate the message that Jesus Christ is the Savior of mankind, and that the kingdom of God is close by.

Deuteronomy 13:1-4 gives the same warning: *"If a prophet arises among you, or a dreamer of dreams, and gives you a sign or a wonder, and the sign or the wonder which he spoke (foretold) to you comes to pass, and if he says, 'Let us follow after other gods (whom you have not known) and let us serve and worship them,' you shall not listen to the words of that prophet or that dreamer of dreams; for the LORD your God is testing you to know whether you love the LORD your God with all your heart and mind and all your soul [your entire being]. You shall walk after the LORD your God and you shall fear [and worship] Him [with awe-filled reverence and profound respect], and you shall keep His commandments and you shall listen to His voice, and you shall serve Him, and cling to Him.*

To attribute Jesus miracles to the prince of demons, is blasphemy against the Holy Spirit and there is no forgiveness. *"I assure you and most solemnly say to you, all sins will be forgiven the sons of men, and all the abusive and blasphemous things they say; but whoever blasphemes against the Holy Spirit and His power [by attributing the miracles done by Me to the evil one] never has forgiveness, but is guilty of an everlasting sin [a sin which is unforgivable in this present age as well as in the age to come]"— [Jesus said this] because the scribes and Pharisees were [attributing His miracles to the evil one by] saying, "He has an unclean spirit." Mark 3:28-30.*

Dr. Kevin Zadai wrote the book "The Mystery of the Power Words" in which He mentions 20+ Power words that must be included in the message of the gospel of Jesus Christ.

If they are left out, rest assured the signs and wonders are false.

Many religious groups mention "God" but fail to actually mention the name of Jesus. They also pray "in your name" but they don't actually say JESUS which is the only name above all names.

SOME "greater works" have been seen throughout the history of the church performed by those who have embraced the complete finished work of Jesus and the resurrection power of the Holy Spirit. Brethren like John G Lake, A A Allen, Bob Jones, Katherine Khulman, Smith Wigglesworth, Mariah Woodrowth-Etter, Roland and Heidi Baker, Madame Jeanne Guyon, Kenneth E Hagin, Bobbie Conner, William and Catherine Booth, William Branham, Aimee Semple McPherson, Kenneth Copeland, T L Osborne, John Wesley, Peter Wagner, Frances Metcalfe, R W Shamback, Benny Hinn, Reinhard Bonnke, John G Lake, David Herzog, Ruth Heflin, Henry Gruver, Cindy Jacobs, Mario Murillo, etc… They all have loved and love the Lord with all their heart, mind, and strength, so the signs and wonders followed them. These lovers of the Lord are too many to mention them all but too few compared to the amount of believers in Christ Jesus around the world.

Jesus said ANYONE not "only a few": *I assure you and most solemnly say to you, **anyone** who believes in Me [as Savior] will also do the things that I do; and he **will do even greater things than these** [in extent and outreach], because I am going to the*

THE GREATER WORKS

97

Father. And I will do whatever you ask in My name [as My representative], this I will do, so that the Father may be glorified and celebrated in the Son. If you ask Me anything in My name [as My representative], I will do it. "If you [really] love Me, you will keep and obey My commandments. John 14:12-15.

Isaiah 55:11 says: *So will My word be which goes out of My mouth; It will not return to Me void (useless, without result), Without accomplishing what I desire, And without succeeding in the matter for which I sent it.*

Father God will not send Jesus back until His word about the greater works succeeds. It's up to us to believe and pursue His presence and to boldly proclaim that the kingdom of God is truly at hand by believing the gospel of salvation through Jesus Christ, and understanding and embracing the power of the resurrection and the authority of the believers.

CHAPTER 9

THE EARTH WILL BE FILLED WITH THE KNOWLEDGE OF THE GLORY OF THE LORD

*"For the vision is yet for the appointed [future] time It hurries toward the goal [of fulfillment]; **it will not fail**. Even though it delays, wait [patiently] for it, Because it will certainly come; it will not delay... "But [the time is coming when] **the earth shall be filled with the knowledge of the glory of the** Lord, As the waters cover the sea. Habakkuk 2:3, 14.*

So the Lord *said, "I have pardoned them according to your word; but indeed as I live, **all the earth will be filled with the glory of the** Lord. Surely all the men who have seen My glory and My [miraculous] signs which I performed in Egypt and in the wilderness, Num 14:20-22.*

In the garden of Eden, it pleased God to be with Adam and Eve, He came down every day to fellowship with them. Adam and Eve enjoyed such closeness to God that they were incredibly radiant beings, full of the light and glory of God, their spirits were alive and their bodies were youthful and didn't age because they ate the fruit of the tree of life, they were not meant to die. But when they disobeyed God, the close personal relationship with God was broken and because of their instant separation from God their spirits died, their light dimmed so they knew they were naked, the glory of God on them had departed. Everything God had created on the earth was cursed and because God's glory wasn't there anymore everything started to decay.

Nonetheless the Lord God continued desiring fellowship with men and ever since has been reachable to those who diligently seek Him and desire to truly know Him.

and I will dwell in their midst forever. Ezek 43:9b.

Come close to God [with a contrite heart] and He will come close to you. James 4:8a.

In the Old Testament in the Bible, we read how the glory of God was visible when God was present. Even when He toned it down, it was an awesome and fearful sight that made the Israelites tremble in terror. We read descriptions of what God's glory looked like at times.

Here I picture God's glory looking like sapphire color northern lights:

Then Moses, Aaron, Nadab, and Abihu, and seventy of the elders of Israel went up [the mountainside], and they saw [a manifestation of] the God of Israel; and under His feet there appeared to be a pavement of sapphire, just as clear as the sky itself. Yet He did not stretch out His hand against the nobles of the Israelites; and they saw [the manifestation of the presence of] God, and ate and drank. Exo 24:9-10.

The glory of God looked like a consuming fire, like the burning bush but amplified.

Now the LORD said to Moses, "Come up to Me on the mountain and stay there, and I will give you the stone tablets with the law and the commandments which I have written for their instruction." So Moses arose with Joshua his attendant, and he went up to the mountain of God. And he said to the elders, "Wait here for us until we come back to you. Remember that Aaron and Hur are with you; whoever has a legal matter, let him go to them." Then Moses went up to the mountain, and the cloud covered the mountain. The glory and brilliance of the LORD rested on Mount Sinai, and the cloud covered it for six days. On the seventh day God called to Moses from the midst of the cloud. In the sight of the Israelites the appearance of the glory and brilliance of the LORD was like consuming fire on the top of the mountain. Moses entered the midst of the cloud and went up the mountain; and he was on the mountain forty days and forty nights. Exo 24:11-18.

The whole nation of Israel saw the glory of the Lord.

*When you heard the voice from the darkness while **the mountain was blazing**, all the leaders and elders of your tribes came to me and said: '**The LORD our God truly has displayed his glory and power,** for we heard him from out of the fire today. We have witnessed how God spoke to human beings, yet they lived. Deut 5:23-24.*

After Moses spent 40 days in God's presence, his countenance was so radiant that he had to cover his face before the people. Can you imagine how radiant were Adam and Eve when they had fellowship with God in the garden?

When Moses came down from Mount Sinai, he had the two tablets in his hand, and he did not know that the skin of his face was ablaze with light because he had been speaking with God. Aaron and all the Israelis saw Moses and immediately noticed that the skin of his face was shining, and they were afraid to come near him. Exo 34:29-30.

God was in the cloud and the pillar of fire:

***The [presence of the] LORD was** going before them by day **in** a pillar (column) of cloud to lead them along the way, and **in** a pillar of fire by night to give them light, so that they could travel by day and by night. He did not withdraw the pillar of cloud by day, nor the pillar of fire by night, from going before the people. Exo 13:21-22.*

Isaiah prophesied that the glory of the Lord will be seen again from Mount Zion.

...then the LORD will create over the entire site of Mount Zion and over her assemblies, a cloud by day, smoke, and the brightness of a flaming fire by night; for over all the glory and brilliance will be a canopy [a defense, a covering of His divine love and protection]. And there will be a pavilion for shade from the heat by day, and a refuge and a shelter from the storm and the rain. Isaiah 4:5-6.

Isaiah was a prophet around 700 years after Moses led Israel out of Egypt so the prophecy is not talking about what Israel experienced in the wilderness but a future event from Mount Zion and over her assemblies. Hebrews 12:18-24 talks about the body of Christ and Mount Zion in the spiritual realm that transcends to the physical, BUT Isaiah's prophecy refers to God's glory manifesting again on the earth because in heaven there are no shadows, no scorching heat, and no one needs shelter and refuge from storms and rain.

Moses saw the real tabernacle in heaven and was commanded to make a replica and to place it in the middle of their camp (read Exodus 25:40). When it was finished, the glory of God sat in the ark and over the tabernacle of meeting.

The cloud covered the Tent of Meeting, and the glory of the LORD filled the tent. Moses was not able to enter the Tent of Meeting because the cloud had settled on it, and the glory of the LORD filled the tent. Exo 40:34-34.

Because Moses spent time in the presence of God, his body didn't age like an average man.

Although Moses was a hundred and twenty years old when he died, his eyesight was not dim, nor his natural strength abated. Deut 34:7.

Even though the people of Israel did not come close to God like Moses and Joshua, the presence of God in the cloud and the pillar of fire was enough to:

[Moses said] I have led you in the wilderness forty years; your clothes have not worn out on you, and your sandals have not worn out on your feet. You have not eaten bread, nor have you drunk wine or strong drink, so that you might know that I am the LORD your God [on whom you must depend]. Deut 29:5-6.

During the time of kings David and Solomon, the glory of God was well known. Later on when the nation of Israel sinned greatly against the Lord, the glory of God departed like we read in Ezekiel 10.

King David was well acquainted with God's glory and presence and so were the people of Israel. Just like Moses, David saw heaven and was shown the future. We know this because of the mention and description of God's glory in the psalms of David (as well as the mention of the Savior, things of heaven and the sufferings of Jesus.)

The voice of the LORD was heard above the waters; the God of glory thundered; the LORD was heard over many waters. Psalm of David 29:3.

Be exalted above the heavens, O God; Let Your glory and majesty be over all the earth. Psalm of David 57:5.

So I have gazed upon You in the sanctuary, To see Your power and Your glory. Psalm of David 63:2.

Blessed be His glorious name forever; And may the whole earth be filled with His glory. Amen and Amen. Psalm of Solomon 72:19.

Be exalted [in majesty], O God, above the heavens, And Your glory above all the earth. Psalm of David 108:5.

They will sing about the ways of the LORD, for great is the glory of the LORD! Psalm of David 138:5.

They shall speak of the glory of Your kingdom And talk of Your power, To make known to the sons of men Your mighty acts and the glorious majesty of Your kingdom. Psalm of David 145:11-12.

As soon as Solomon finished his prayer, fire descended from heaven and burned up the burnt offerings and sacrifices, and the glory of the LORD filled the Temple. The priests could not enter into the Temple because the glory of the LORD had filled the LORD's Temple. When all of the Israelites saw the fire coming down and the glory of the LORD resting on the Temple, they bowed down

THE EARTH WILL BE FILLED WITH THE KNOWLEDGE OF THE GLORY OF THE LORD   105 *with their faces to the ground on the pavement, worshiped, and gave thanks to the LORD. 2 Chron 7:1-3.*

It has always been God's desire to manifest His glory among His people, that is one of the things the enemies of God and His people noticed and feared. The visible manifestation of God's glory is not to put up a show to look at, it is His visible presence with all his attributes. In His glory, the Israelites were: protected from their enemies, kept from the weather, fed, provided, kept healthy, saw and experienced miracles, and would have felt God's love if they had submitted themselves to His goodness. It is God's desire to show His people His glory and to live with them.

What is man that you take notice of him, or the son of man that you pay attention to him? You made him a little less than divine, but you crowned him with glory and honor. Psalm of David 8:4-5.

And [the LORD] said to Me, "You are My Servant, Israel, In Whom I will show My glory." Isa 49:3.

"And the glory and majesty and splendor of the LORD will be revealed, And all humanity shall see it together; For the mouth of the LORD has spoken it." Isa 40:5.

"Then your light will break out like the dawn, And your healing (restoration, new life) will quickly spring forth; Your righteousness will go before you [leading you to peace and prosperity], The glory of the LORD will be your rear guard. Isa 58:8.

You will also be [considered] a crown of glory and splendor in the hand of the LORD, And a royal diadem [exceedingly beautiful] in the hand of your God. Isa 62:3.

Many scriptures in the Bible have more than one revelation. They are descriptions of some things of heaven, figures of things to come, historical information of things in the past, shadows of God's kingdom. Holy Spirit's revelation of such things is needed to understand and to interpret the time we live in.

There is a real spiritual tabernacle in heaven where the real mercy seat is, where Jesus sprinkled His blood when He first ascended to the Father.

Jesus said to her (Mary), "Do not hold Me, for I have not yet ascended to the Father; but go to My brothers and tell them, 'I am ascending to My Father and your Father, and to My God and your God.'" John 20:17.

Jesus told Mary that He had to ascend to His Father before He could be touched. Hundreds of **years earlier** Daniel saw what happened when Jesus ascended to the Father:

"I kept looking in the night visions, And behold, on the clouds of heaven One like a Son of Man was coming, And He came up to the Ancient of Days And was presented before Him. "And to Him (the Messiah) was given dominion (supreme authority), Glory and a kingdom, That all the peoples, nations, and speakers of every language should serve and worship Him. His dominion is an

everlasting dominion which will not pass away; and His kingdom is one which will not be destroyed. Daniel 7:13-14.

Then, **years after** Jesus ascended to His Father, the writer of the book of Hebrews saw that scene too.

But when Christ appeared as a High Priest of the good things to come [that is, true spiritual worship], He entered through the greater and more perfect tabernacle, not made with hands, that is to say, not a part of this [material] creation. He went once for all into the Holy Place [the Holy of Holies of heaven, into the presence of God], and not through the blood of goats and calves, but through His own blood, having obtained and secured eternal redemption [that is, the salvation of all who personally believe in Him as Savior]. Hebrews 9:11-12.

Therefore it was necessary for the [earthly] copies of the heavenly things to be cleansed with these, but the heavenly things themselves required far better sacrifices than these. For Christ did not enter into a holy place made with hands, a mere copy of the true one, but [He entered] into heaven itself, now to appear in the very presence of God on our behalf; Heb 9:23-24.

Once we grasp the revelation through the spirit of Wisdom and Understanding, we can see that the promises of God's glory over Israel are the same over His people born again through faith in Jesus Christ. The blessings of Abraham are also for the born again believers in Christ. The blessings of the Old Covenant are not taken away but added to the blessing in the new covenant in Christ's blood.

When Moses asked the Lord "show me your glory" in Exodus 33:18-20 the Lord showed him His goodness in Exodus 34:5-8. God's glory or presence carries all the attributes of God in it.

Then Moses said, "Please, show me Your glory!" And God said, "I will make all My goodness pass before you, and I will proclaim the Name of the LORD before you; for I will be gracious to whom I will be gracious, and will show compassion (lovingkindness) on whom I will show compassion." But He said, "You cannot see My face, for no [sinful/fallen] man shall see Me and live!"

Then the LORD descended in the cloud and stood there with Moses as he proclaimed the Name of the LORD. Then the LORD passed by in front of him, and proclaimed, "The LORD, the LORD God, compassionate and gracious, slow to anger, and abounding in lovingkindness and truth (faithfulness); keeping mercy and lovingkindness for thousands, forgiving iniquity and transgression and sin; but He will by no means leave the guilty unpunished, visiting (avenging) the iniquity (sin, guilt) of the fathers upon the children and the grandchildren to the third and fourth generations [that is, calling the children to account for the sins of their fathers]." Moses bowed to the earth immediately and worshiped [the Lord].

The Lord promises that the glory of the Lord will be in His tabernacle or temple:

For thus says the LORD of hosts, 'Once more, in a little while, I am going to shake the heavens and the earth, the sea and the *dry land. I will shake all the nations; and they will come with the desirable and precious things of all nations, **and I will fill this house with glory and splendor,'** says the* L ORD *of hosts. 'The silver is Mine and the gold is Mine,' declares the* L ORD *of hosts. **'The latter glory of this house will be greater than the former,'** says the* L ORD *of hosts, 'and in this place I shall give [the ultimate] peace and prosperity,' declares the* L ORD *of hosts." Haggai 2:6-9.*

NOW the body of Christ (the church) is the Temple of God.

*Do you not know and understand that **you** [the church] **are the temple of God**, and that the Spirit of God dwells [permanently] in you [collectively and individually]? If anyone destroys the temple of God [corrupting it with false doctrine], God will destroy the destroyer; for the temple of God is holy (sacred), and that is what **you** are. 1 Cor 3:16-17.*

If God showed His glory (goodness, protection, sustenance, etc) to a rebellious and stiff necked people, would He not manifest Himself in those bought by His Son's own blood?

Arise [from spiritual depression to a new life], shine [be radiant with the glory and brilliance of the L ORD*]; for your light has come, And the glory and brilliance of the* L ORD *has risen upon you. "For in fact, darkness will cover the earth And deep darkness will cover the peoples; But the* L ORD *will rise upon you [Jerusalem] and His glory and brilliance will be seen on you... "The sun will no longer be your light by day, Nor shall the bright glow of the moon give light to you, But the* L ORD *will be an* *everlasting light for you; and your God will be your glory and splendor. Isa 60:1-2, 19.*

Even though the glory of the Lord had departed from Israel long time ago (as we read in Ezekiel 10 how the cherubim took God's glory back to heaven), the shepherds saw it when Jesus was born.

An angel of the Lord appeared to them (the shepherds), and the glory of the Lord shone around them, and they were terrified. Luke 2:9.

Jesus, at times, let His disciples see God's glory.

*And the Word (Christ) became flesh, and lived among us; **and we [actually] saw His glory**, glory as belongs to the [One and] only begotten Son of the Father, [the Son who is truly unique, the only One of His kind, who is] full of grace and truth (absolutely free of deception). John 1:14.*

Once more Jesus addressed the crowd. He said, "I am the Light of the world. He who follows Me will not walk in the darkness, but will have the Light of life." John 8:12.

Some disciples saw Jesus' glory in the mount of transfiguration.

Now about eight days after these teachings, He took along Peter and John and James and went up on the mountain to pray. As He was praying, the appearance of His face became different [actually transformed], and His clothing became white and flashing with the brilliance of lightning. And behold, two men were talking with Him; and they were Moses and Elijah, who appeared in glory, and were speaking of His departure [from earthly life], which He was about to bring to fulfillment at Jerusalem. Now Peter and those who were with him had been overcome with sleep; but when they were fully awake, they saw His glory and splendor and majesty, and the two men who were standing with Him. And as these [men, Moses and Elijah] were leaving Him, Peter said to Jesus, "Master, it is delightful and good for us to be here; we should make three [sacred] tents; one for You, one for Moses, and one for Elijah"—not realizing what he was saying. But even as he was saying this, a cloud formed and began to overshadow them; and they were [greatly] afraid as they entered the cloud. Then a voice came out of the cloud, saying, "This is My beloved Son, My Chosen One; listen and obey and yield to Him!" When the voice had ceased, Jesus was found there alone. And they kept silent, and told no one at that time any of the things which they had seen [concerning the divine manifestation]. Luke 9:28-36.

Jesus prayed to Father God to give all who will ever believe in Jesus to give them the glory He had given His disciples. It is not a future in heaven request but to support the gospel of salvation here and now.

"I do not pray for these alone [it is not for their sake only that I make this request], but also for [all] those who [will ever] believe and trust in Me through their message, that they all may be one; just as You, Father, are in Me and I in You, that they

*also may be one in Us, **so that the world may believe [with-
out any doubt] that You sent Me. I have given to them the
glory and honor which You have given Me**, that they may
be one, just as We are one; **I in them** and You in Me, that they
may be perfected and completed into one, so that the world may
know [without any doubt] that You sent Me, and [that You]
have loved them, just as You have loved Me. Father, I desire that
they also, whom You have given to Me [as Your gift to Me], may
be with Me where I am, so that they may see My glory which You
have given Me, because You loved Me before the foundation of
the world. John 17:20-24.*

Jesus talked about it as being light. The works are not the
light, it is His glory upon His people but it will only manifest
in the measure we are transformed into the likeness of Jesus.

*You are the light of [Christ to] the world. A city set on a hill
cannot be hidden; nor does anyone light a lamp and put it
under a basket, but on a lampstand, and it gives light to all
who are in the house. Let your light shine before men in such
a way that they may see your good deeds and moral excellence,
and [recognize and honor and] glorify your Father who is in
heaven. "Do not think that I came to do away with or undo
the Law [of Moses] or the [writings of the] Prophets; I did
not come to destroy but to fulfill. For I assure you and most
solemnly say to you, until heaven and earth pass away, not the
smallest letter or stroke [of the pen] will pass from the Law
until all things [which it foreshadows] are accomplished*.
Matthew 5:14-18.

We have seen for ourselves and can testify that the Father has sent his Son to be the Savior of the world. **God abides in the one who acknowledges that Jesus is the Son of God, and he abides in God.** *We have come to know and rely on the love that God has for us. God is love, and the person who abides in love abides in God, and God abides in him. This is how love has been perfected among us: we will have confidence on the day of judgment because,* **during our time in this world, we are just like him.** *1 John 4:14-17.*

The writer of Hebrews also talks about God's glory:

The Son (Jesus) is the radiance and only expression of the glory of [our awesome] God [reflecting God's Shekinah glory, the Light-being, the brilliant light of the divine], and the exact representation and perfect imprint of His [Father's] essence, Hebrews 1:3a.

The glory of God was present at different times but the people had hardened hearts and could not recognize it, just like the people of Israel only saw a cloud and a pillar of fire instead of the presence of God, in the time of Jesus people only heard thunder and did not see the heavens open above them. Now days, part of the church is dull, they are so hardened that can't recognize God's presence. They desire the glory, but are not willing to pay the price of living completely holy lives surrendered and led of the Holy Spirit, if the glory shows up they will not be able to survive. When God really shows up there are visible tangible manifestations of His presence/glory, being the Fear of the Lord one of them. When the glory of the Lord shows up, there's great conviction of sin because

He is holy. Many people fall on their faces and worship God.

When the day of Pentecost was being celebrated, all of them were together in one place. Suddenly, a sound like the roar of a mighty windstorm came from heaven and filled the whole house where they were sitting. They saw tongues like flames of fire that separated, and one rested on each of them. All of them were filled with the Holy Spirit and began to speak in foreign languages as the Spirit gave them that ability. Acts 2:1-4.

God's glory includes His physical manifestation AND His goodness. The glory/goodness of the Lord will be seen and known in all the world because His children [God's tabernacle/house/ dwelling place] will carry it with them. The will look, smell, walk, talk like Jesus did when He walked the earth.

The Bible has many examples in the old and new testaments of people who saw God:

Enoch   Genesis 5:24

Noah   Genesis 6:9

Abraham   Genesis 18:1-33

Jacob   Genesis 32:30

Moses, Aron and 70 elders of Israel   Exodus 24:9-11

Moses and Joshua   Exodus 33:11

Moses	Numbers 12:7,8
All Israel	Deuteronomy 5:4
Isaiah	Isaiah 6:1
Job	Job 42:5
Ezekiel	Ezekiel 1:26-28
Daniel	Daniel 7:9-10, 13-14
Amos	Amos 9:1
David	Acts 2:25
Stephen	Acts 7:55-56
Paul	2 Corinthians 12:2-4; Galatians 1:12
John	Revelation 1:8-18; 4

Some of those in the Old Testament who saw the LORD, walked and talked to God were not born again in Christ children of God, yet they desired to know Him and pursued Him in such a way that God was pleased with them. To others, God Himself reached out to them and they responded with great faith and devotion to Him.

Immature Christians don't understand the scriptures that say "no one has seen God" or "no one can see God and live" or "no man can see God and live". These verses are talking about sinful men, unredeemed people. The apostle's letters clearly explain that the born again believers are not "mere humans" anymore, but New Creatures, citizens of heaven, carriers of God. God's children are continually reminded that they ought not behave like mere mortals anymore but to completely change into the likeness of Jesus Christ. God's children are expected to approach boldly the throne of God's grace.

There have been some brothers and sisters in the Body of Christ that have been in God's presence, taken to the third heaven or have been visited by God, and His glory remains on them for a while like Rev. Jesse Duplantis. I am not saying ALL believers will manifest God's glory, but there will be a lot of believers that will walk so close to God that the whole earth will know about it. Like the Levites, the carriers of the glory of God will be able to stand and minister in God's presence.

There have been times in church meetings that the glory of God appears like a canopy of fire in such a visible way that the neighbors call the fire department.

The apostle Paul explained that the glory of the Lord is about to be revealed to us and in us, among other things, to free the whole creation from frustration, futility, decay, and bondage to bring it into the glorious freedom of the children of God.

THE EARTH WILL BE FILLED WITH THE KNOWLEDGE OF THE GLORY OF THE LORD 117

This is clearly a matter that pertains to the earth and it can only be accomplished when the glory of the Lord is revealed to and in God's children. As New Creatures in Christ we are groaning and eagerly waiting for the ultimate part of our transformation into the likeness of Jesus which is a glorified body. In our growth and our close walk with God we go "from glory to glory", our Heavenly Father gives us measures of glory so that we are not destroyed by it.

*Romans 8:18-23 For I consider [from the standpoint of faith] that the sufferings of the present life are not worthy to be compared with **the glory that is about to be revealed to us and in us**! For [even the whole] creation [all nature] waits eagerly for the children of God to be revealed. For the creation was subjected to frustration and futility, not willingly [because of some intentional fault on its part], but by the will of Him who subjected it, in hope that the creation itself will also be freed from its bondage to decay [and gain entrance] into the glorious freedom of the children of God. For we know that the whole creation has been moaning together as in the pains of childbirth until now. And not only this, but we too, who have the first fruits of the Spirit [a joyful indication of the blessings to come], even we groan inwardly, as we wait eagerly for [the sign of] our adoption as sons—the redemption and transformation of our body [at the resurrection].*

God's glory is His presence. The body of Christ has to passionately wait on Him, meditate on His Word, diligently seek Him and draw near to Him, recognize the Awesomeness of

God, humble itself before Him. Stop talking and complaining and wait for Him to talk, to instruct, to reveal, to love and to sing over us. Waiting on Him will hardly happen in a pre-ordained church service where there's a set time for each activity where Holy Spirit doesn't have freedom to do what He wants when He wants to. Our Holy God is available and willing but He will never move at our pace neither will He submit to our agendas. Because our lives are not ours anymore, His presence will manifest when the body of Christ learns to crucify the flesh and separates itself for God. There must be heartfelt brokenness and constant repentance turning back to God.

Until the whole earth is filled with the knowledge of the glory of God, Jesus can not come back.

CHAPTER 10

THE POWERS OF THE AGE TO COME

*...those who have once been enlightened [spiritually] and who have tasted and consciously experienced the heavenly gift and have shared in the Holy Spirit, and have tasted and consciously experienced the good word of God **and the powers of the age (world) to come**, Heb 6:4b-5*

Hebrews 6:1-8 explains that the believers in Christ Jesus must advance in the maturity process to go from Teknon (immature son/daughter living in full dependence of the parents) to Huios (son/daughter that has matured and shares the same nature, character, and becomes like the parents).

Concerning this we have much to say, and it is hard to explain, since you have become dull and sluggish in [your spiritual] *hearing and disinclined to listen. For though by this time you ought to be teachers [because of the time you have had to learn these truths], you actually need someone to teach you again the elementary principles of God's word [from the beginning], and you have come to be continually in need of milk, not solid food. For everyone who lives on milk is [doctrinally inexperienced and] unskilled in the word of righteousness, since he is a spiritual infant. **But solid food is for the [spiritually] mature, whose senses are trained by practice to distinguish between what is morally good and what is evil.** Hebrews 5:11-14.*

Jesus told His disciples they were not mature yet, they didn't have revelation about the things of God, but then Jesus goes on to say that Holy Spirit will reveal the things of God.

"I have many more things to say to you, but you cannot bear [to hear] them now. But when He, the Spirit of Truth, comes, He will guide you into all the truth [full and complete truth]. For He will not speak on His own initiative, but He will speak whatever He hears [from the Father—the message regarding the Son], and He will disclose to you what is to come [in the future]. He will glorify and honor Me, because He (the Holy Spirit) will take from what is Mine and will disclose it to you. All things that the Father has are Mine. Because of this I said that He [the Spirit] will take from what is Mine and will reveal it to you. John 16:12-15.

The apostle Paul addressed the saints as "little children" and he said: *I could not talk to you as to spiritual people, but [only] as to worldly people [dominated by human nature], mere infants [in the new life] in Christ! I fed you with milk, not solid food; for you were not yet able to receive it. Even now you are still not ready. 1 Corinthians 3:1b-2.*

Believers born again in Jesus Christ are called to move from "new born" to "total dependence on Father God, Jesus and His Holy Spirit" to "become mature sons/daughters like Jesus".

The apostle John explains:

*And this is how we know [daily, by experience] that we have come to know Him [to understand Him and be more deeply acquainted with Him]: if we habitually keep [focused on His precepts and obey] His commandments (teachings). Whoever says, "I have come to know Him," but does not habitually keep [focused on His precepts and obey] His commandments (teachings), is a liar, and the truth [of the divine word] is not in him. <u>But whoever habitually keeps His word and obeys His precepts [and treasures His message in its entirety], in him the love of God has truly been perfected [it is completed **and has reached maturity**]</u>. By this we know [for certain] that we are in Him: whoever says he lives in Christ [that is, whoever says he has accepted Him as God and Savior] ought [as a moral obligation] to walk and conduct himself just as He (Jesus) walked and conducted Himself. 1 John 2:3-6.*

And the apostle Peter says:

Therefore, [let me warn you] beloved, knowing these things beforehand, be on your guard so that you are not carried away *by the error of unprincipled men [who distort doctrine] and fall from your own steadfastness [of mind, knowledge, truth, and faith], but grow [**spiritually mature**] in the grace and knowledge of our Lord and Savior Jesus Christ. To Him be glory (honor, majesty, splendor), both now and to the day of eternity. Amen. 2 Peter 3:17-18.*

No immature heir (no matter how wealthy the family is or how well known and respected the parents are) is trusted with the rule and administration of the estate and even more so if the heir is to inherit the royal crown. That child has to mature and also has to be trained and taught in all matters that pertain to the palace, foreign affairs, and the whole kingdom (people, land, and all resources). He/she has to develop character to be entrusted to ultimately rule over all his/her inheritance.

Proverbs 31:1-5, 8-9 describes a righteous ruler:

What, O my son? And what, O son of my womb? And what [shall I advise you], O son of my vows? Do not give your [generative] strength to women [neither foreign wives in marriages of alliances, nor concubines], Nor your ways to that which destroys kings. It is not for kings, O Lemuel, It is not for kings to drink wine, Or for rulers to desire strong drink, Otherwise they drink and forget the law and its decrees, And pervert the rights and justice of all the afflicted... Open your mouth for the mute, For the rights of all who are unfortunate and defenseless; Open your mouth, judge righteously, And administer justice for the afflicted and needy.

A believer in Christ Jesus will mature by the revelation of the Word of God by the Holy Spirit.

Yet we do speak wisdom among those **spiritually mature** *[believers who have teachable hearts and a greater understanding]; but [it is a higher] wisdom not [the wisdom] of this present age nor of the rulers and leaders of this age, who are passing away; but we speak God's wisdom in a mystery, the wisdom once hidden [from man, but now revealed to us by God, that wisdom] which God predestined before the ages to our glory [to lift us into the glory of His presence]. None of the rulers of this age recognized and understood this wisdom; for if they had, they would not have crucified the Lord of glory; but just as it is written [in Scripture],*

"THINGS WHICH THE EYE HAS NOT SEEN AND THE EAR HAS NOT HEARD, AND WHICH HAVE NOT ENTERED THE HEART OF MAN, ALL THAT GOD HAS PREPARED FOR THOSE WHO LOVE HIM [who hold Him in affectionate reverence, who obey Him, and who gratefully recognize the benefits that He has bestowed]."

For God has unveiled them and revealed them to us through the [Holy] Spirit; for the Spirit searches all things [diligently], even [sounding and measuring] the [profound] depths of God [the divine counsels and things far beyond human understanding]. For what person knows the thoughts and motives of a man except the man's spirit within him? So also no one knows the thoughts of God except the Spirit of God. Now we have received, not the spirit of the world, but the [Holy] Spirit who is from God, so that we may know and understand the [wonderful] things freely given to us by God. We also speak of these things, not in words taught or supplied by human wisdom, but in those taught by the Spirit, combining and interpreting spiritual thoughts with spiritual words [for those being guided by the Holy Spirit].

*But the natural [unbelieving] man does not accept the things [the teachings and revelations] of the Spirit of God, for they are foolishness [absurd and illogical] to him; and he is incapable of understanding them, because they are spiritually discerned and appreciated, [and he is unqualified to judge spiritual matters]. But the spiritual man [**the spiritually mature Christian**] judges all things [questions, examines and applies what the Holy Spirit reveals], yet is himself judged by no one [the unbeliever cannot judge and understand the believer's spiritual nature]. For WHO HAS KNOWN THE MIND and PURPOSES OF THE LORD, SO AS TO INSTRUCT HIM? But we have the mind of Christ [to be guided by His thoughts and purposes]. 1 Cor 2:6-16.*

It takes revelation of the Word of God to experience God to become mature sons of God.

For all who are allowing themselves to be led by the Spirit of God are sons (huios) of God. Rom 8:14.

Any person can read and repeat the Bible, the evil one knows it enough to twist it, the unbelievers can't understand it, born again believers read it and often times they perceive it as a history or story book but they can't relate to it or barely understand it because it takes the Holy Spirit to bring it to life.

A good way to have revelation is, first of all to ask Jesus for the baptism of Holy Spirit and Fire like He sent His Spirit at Pentecost, then ask Father God for the spirit of wisdom and revelation in the knowledge of God like the apostle Paul used to pray:

([I always pray] that the God of our Lord Jesus Christ, the Father of glory, may grant you a spirit of wisdom and of revelation [that gives you a deep and personal and intimate insight] into the true knowledge of Him [for we know the Father through the Son]. Eph 1:17.

Then read the Bible until you have a "WOW!" moment, then stop and meditate (think about) that Bible verse or passage. Once you understand it and it is established in your heart (made alive and you can relate to it) then you can move on reading the Bible.

Every time you have questions about the Bible, ask the Holy Spirit a specific question and read the passage again, it helps to have a Bible with references. God is a relational, personal God. He will speak the language you are comfortable with, for instance: if you are a computer geek He will explain things to you in computer terms. If you are a cook, He will use culinary terms to help you understand. If you are a plumber, He will use plumbing terms and examples so you can relate to it. Printed Study Bibles are good for information but Holy Spirit is much better for relationship. The apostle John explains:

As for you, the anointing [the special gift, the preparation] which you received from Him remains [permanently] in you, and you have no need for anyone to teach you. But just as His anointing teaches you [giving you insight through the presence of the Holy Spirit] about all things, and is true and is not a lie, and just as His anointing has taught you, you must remain in Him [being rooted in Him, knit to Him]. 1 John 2:27.

The work of the five fold ministry is to the church, to the body of Christ as a whole. The Apostles, Prophets, Teachers, Evangelists and Pastors are gifts from Jesus:

*...to fully equip and perfect the saints (God's people) for works of service, to build up the body of Christ [the church]; <u>until we all reach oneness in the faith and in the knowledge of the Son of God, [growing spiritually]</u> **to become a mature believer**, <u>reaching to the measure of the fullness of Christ [manifesting His spiritual completeness and exercising our spiritual gifts in unity]. Eph 4:12b-13.</u>*

Revelation and the personal teaching of the Holy Spirit is relational between God and the believer, so that the believer gets to actually know God and not only know *about* God. It is in this personal relationship that the believer learns to recognize God's voice, and starts to trust Him more and more. Only then the believer is on the way to become spiritually mature. God and the believer spend time together, discovering the mysteries and treasures in the Word of God, leaning on Holy Spirit in every circumstance, knowing that God turns everything into good because there's mutual deep love between them.

Once God gets to trust His mature son/daughter, He starts allowing him/her to see, experience and walk in the greater, deeper, supernatural things of God.

We read in the Bible how God desires to reveal secrets to His people.

Moses was shown how creation happened, not only the universe but the creation of man and the genealogies after Adam and Eve and their stories. That's how and why Moses could write the book of Genesis. He was also taken to the third heaven, where God's throne is and he was commanded to make a replica (much smaller than the original in heaven) called the Tent or Tabernacle of meeting including the ark of the covenant and the mercy seat where the blood of the sacrifice was sprinkled. It is on the real mercy seat in heaven where Jesus brought His own blood as the ultimate acceptable sacrifice to redeem mankind to God. There's no and will never be need for blood sacrifices anymore.

(Moses) See that you make them [exactly] after their pattern which was shown to you on the mountain. Exo 25:40.

The secret things belong to the LORD our God, but the things which are revealed and disclosed belong to us and to our children forever. Deut 29:29.

God speaks not only through an inner voice or inspiration but by visions, spiritual encounters and real face to face encounters.

The LORD *said, "Shall I keep secret from Abraham [My friend and servant] what I am going to do. Gen 18:17.*

I will stand at my guard post and station myself on the tower; And I will keep watch **to see what He will say** *to me, and what answer I will give [as His spokesman] when I am reproved. Hab 2:1.*

Call to Me and I will answer you, and tell you [and even show you] great and mighty things, [things which have been confined and hidden], which you do not know and understand and cannot distinguish. Jer 33:3.

It is He who reveals the profound and hidden things; He knows what is in the darkness, and the light dwells with Him. Daniel 2:22.

Surely the Lord GOD *does nothing without revealing His secret plan [of the judgment to come] to His servants the prophets. Amos 3:7.*

I do not call you servants any longer, for the servant does not know what his master is doing; but I have called you [My] friends, because I have revealed to you everything that I have heard from My Father. John 15:15.

All things that the Father has are Mine. Because of this I said that He [the Spirit] will take from what is Mine and will reveal it to you. John 16:15.

THE POWERS OF THE AGE TO COME

It is in the process of total submission to God trusting Him, being led by His Holy Spirit, and washed by the Word of God that the believer can become more like Jesus, to a mature son and bond-servant of God like Jesus, then the Father can trust the believer with the revelation of the deeper things of God and with the revelation of how to occupy the earth and to make it as it is in heaven. When God created Adam and Eve, that was the original plan for the earth, and we have seen that He hasn't changed His mind. His original intent and purpose has been to make earth to operate like the kingdom of God, uniting both realms – heaven and earth / spiritual and material -in perfect harmony and peace.

God chose to do it through Adam and his descendants (*The heavens are the heavens of the* LORD, ***But the earth He has given to the children of men.*** *Psalm 115:16; and What is man that You are mindful of him, and the son of [earthborn] man that You care for him? Yet You have made him a little lower than God, and You have crowned him with glory and honor.* ***You made him to have dominion over the works of Your hands; You have put all things under his feet***, *Psalm 8:4-8)* but because of disobedience (rebellion/sin) Adam transferred that authority to the evil one. Then Jesus, the second Adam, came and took back the authority and everything that the first Adam lost. The fallen cherubim still had the authority when he tempted Jesus in the wilderness but Jesus took it back *When He had disarmed the rulers and authorities [those supernatural forces of evil operating against us], He made a public example of them [exhibiting them as captives in His* *triumphal procession], having triumphed over them through the cross. Col 2:15.*

Jesus also took the keys of hell and death (*I am the First and the Last [absolute Deity, the Son of God], and the Ever-living One [living in and beyond all time and space]. I died, but see, I am alive forevermore, and I have the keys of [absolute control and victory over] death and of Hades (the realm of the dead). Rev 1:17a-18).*

Jesus gave the commission to "disciple the nations", that is to teach the nations of the earth to operate like the kingdom of God.

Jesus also gave His people the key of David and the keys of the kingdom of God:

"Then I will set on his shoulder the key of the house of David; When he opens no one will shut, When he shuts no one will open. Isaiah 22:22. Remember, Jesus is the head and the church is the body.

I will give you the keys (authority) of the kingdom of heaven; and whatever you bind [forbid, declare to be improper and un-lawful] on earth will have [already] been bound in heaven, and whatever you loose [permit, declare lawful] on earth will have [already] been loosed in heaven." Matt 16:19.

Jesus used binding and losing (releasing) to give us example:

THE POWERS OF THE AGE TO COME   131

And there was a woman who for eighteen years had had an illness caused by a spirit (demon). She was bent double, and could not straighten up at all. When Jesus saw her, He called her over and said to her, **"Woman, you are released (loosed) from your illness."** *Then He laid His hands on her; and immediately she stood erect again and she began glorifying and praising God. Luke 13:11-13.*

The mature sons of God are and will be the ones who have been enlightened [spiritually] and who have tasted *and* consciously experienced the heavenly gift and have shared in the Holy Spirit, and have tasted *and* consciously experienced the good word of God and the powers of the age (world) to come. The age to come will unite heaven and earth, the spiritual with the material. There have already been people who have pursued and believed God in such a way that have tasted it. They go back and forth to heaven while they are alive on earth, they see in the spiritual realm just as they see the material one. They are helped by angels. They get incredible revelation of the past and the future and have great authority in the spirit. They are much more accountable before God for everything they do and the price to pay is very high (total and absolute dependence and obedience to Father God like we read in Jeremiah 10:23 *O Lord, I know that the path of [life of] a man is not in himself; It is not within [the limited ability of] man [even one at his best] to choose and direct his steps [in life].*

Like Jesus: *Jesus answered them by saying, "My teaching is not My own, but His who sent Me. If anyone is willing to do His will, he will know whether the teaching is of God or whether I speak on My own accord and by My own authority. He who speaks on his own accord seeks glory and honor for himself. But He who seeks the glory and the honor of the One who sent Him, He is true, and there is no unrighteousness or deception in Him. John 7:16-18.*

Like James (James 1:1); Peter (2 Peter 1:1); Paul (Rom 1:1).

Paul explains:

*...but just as it is written [in Scripture], THINGS WHICH THE EYE HAS NOT SEEN AND THE EAR HAS NOT HEARD, AND WHICH HAVE NOT ENTERED THE HEART OF MAN, ALL THAT GOD HAS PREPARED FOR THOSE WHO LOVE HIM [who hold Him in affectionate reverence, who obey Him, and who gratefully recognize the benefits that He has bestowed]." **For God has unveiled them and revealed them to us through the [Holy] Spirit; for the Spirit searches all things [diligently], even [sounding and measuring] the [profound] depths of God [the divine counsels and things far beyond human understanding].** *1 Cor 2:9-10.*

...that is, the mystery which was hidden [from angels and mankind] for ages and generations, but has now been revealed to His saints (God's people). Col 1:26.

It is not wise to share everything the sons of God are told and shown by God, He even sometimes tells not to do it. It always has to be initiated and led by Holy Spirit. The believer must trust God and allow Him to decide when and how

THE POWERS OF THE AGE TO COME   133

God wants to do the encounter. If the believer tries to push his way to it he will end up in witchcraft. The spirits always have to be tested to know if the encounter and revelation come from the true Living God or are a counterfeit from the second heaven. Our hearts must be set on Father God, Jesus Christ and Holy Spirit and not on the encounters and/ or revelation. In every encounter we have to ask God for two or three scriptures that back up what was shown to us. Jesus always quoted scripture and He still does. And we have to be very careful not to do the things of the world or the spiritual counterfeit and expect God to protect us.

I know a man in Christ who fourteen years ago—whether in the body I do not know, or out of the body I do not know, [only] God knows—such a man was caught up to the third heaven. And I know that such a man—whether in the body or out of the body I do not know, [only] God knows - was caught up into Paradise and heard inexpressible words **which man is not permitted to speak** *[words too sacred to tell]. 2 Cor 12:2-4.*

but now has been disclosed and through the prophetic Scriptures has been made known to all the nations, according to the commandment of the eternal God, leading them to obedience to the faith, Romans 16:26.

And the angel said, "Go your way, Daniel, for the words are concealed and sealed up until the end of time. Daniel 12:9.

And when the seven peals of thunder had spoken, I was about to write; but I heard a voice from heaven saying, "Seal up the things which the seven peals of thunder have spoken and do not write them down." Rev 10:4.

All the scriptures in the Old and New Testaments are God revealed/inspired.

All Scripture is God-breathed [given by divine inspiration] and is profitable for instruction, for conviction [of sin], for correction [of error and restoration to obedience], for training in righteousness [learning to live in conformity to God's will, both publicly and privately—behaving honorably with personal integrity and moral courage]; so that the man of God may be complete and proficient, outfitted and thoroughly equipped for every good work. 2 Timothy 3:16-17.

We see a few examples of the things God has revealed:

* *The creation of the universe and the history of the birth of Israel. Book of Genesis.*

* *When I see and consider Your heavens, the work of Your fingers, The moon and the stars, which You have established, Psalms 8:3.*

* *Even there Your hand will lead me, And Your right hand will take hold of me. Psalm 139:10.*

* *For You formed my innermost parts; You knit me [together] in my mother's womb. I will give thanks and praise to You, for I am fearfully and wonderfully made; Wonderful are Your works, And my soul knows it very well. My frame was not hidden from*

You, When I was being formed in secret, And intricately and skillfully formed [as if embroidered with many colors] in the depths of the earth. Your eyes have seen my unformed substance; And in Your book were all written The days that were appointed for me, When as yet there was not one of them [even taking shape]. How precious also are Your thoughts to me, O God! How vast is the sum of them! Psalm 139:13-17.

* *He counts the number of the stars; He calls them all by their names. Psalm 147:4.*

* *He made the moon for the seasons; The sun knows the [exact] place of its setting. Psalm 104:19 (read the whole chapter).*

* *Who has measured the waters in the hollow of His hand, And marked off the heavens with a span [of the hand], And calculated the dust of the earth with a measure, And weighed the mountains in a balance And the hills in a pair of scales? Isa 40:12.*

* *It is He who sits above the* **circle** *of the earth* (the earth is not flat), *And its inhabitants are like grasshoppers; [It is He] who stretches out the heavens like a veil And spreads them out like a tent to dwell in. Isa 40:22.*

* *So God said, "Let the earth sprout [tender] vegetation, plants yielding seed, and fruit trees bearing fruit according to (limited to, consistent with) their kind, whose seed is in them upon the earth"; and it was so. The earth sprouted and abundantly produced vegetation, plants yielding seed according to their kind, and trees bearing fruit with seed in them, according to their* *kind; and God saw that it was good and He affirmed and sustained it. Gen 1:11-12.*

* "Ice is made by the breath of God, And the expanse of the waters is frozen. "He loads the thick cloud with moisture; He disperses the cloud of His lightning. "Its direction is turned around by His guidance, That it may do whatever He commands it on the face of the inhabited earth. Job 37:10-12 (read the whole chapter) Read Job 38; 39; 40; 41;

It is in the intimate relationship with God, full of reverential fear of the Lord for His holiness and great power, that God favors His sons and daughters. That favor carries the glory of the Lord in ways spiritual babies can't stand or endure. The favor and glory these sons and daughters of the Most High God manifest affect everything around them in both the spiritual and physical realms. It is in the manifestation of the sons of God that everything will start to look and operate like the kingdom of heaven. Jesus is the head, the church is His body on the earth. Father God is waiting for the body of Christ to understand this and to pursue this relationship with all their hearts, minds and strength, and to be completely led by the Only One Head Jesus. Christ already made available to us all the provision needed for this to happen; He not only became the way to approach Father God with boldness and confidence of acceptance, but He has provided all the supernatural wisdom, power, authority, faith, help, etc., to accomplish it. And He has given us His Holy Spirit to teach, reveal, help and guide us.

*[I always pray] that the God of our Lord Jesus Christ, the Father of glory, may grant you a spirit of wisdom and of revelation [that gives you a deep and personal and intimate insight] into the true knowledge of Him [for we know the Father through the Son]. And [I pray] that the eyes of your heart [the very center and core of your being] may be enlightened [flooded with light by the Holy Spirit], so that you will know and cherish the hope [the divine guarantee, the confident expectation] to which He has called you, the riches of His glorious inheritance in the saints (God's people), and [so that you will begin to know] what the immeasurable and unlimited and surpassing greatness of His [active, spiritual] power **is in us** who believe. These are in accordance with the working of His mighty strength which He produced in Christ when He raised Him from the dead and seated Him at His own right hand in the heavenly places, far above all rule and authority and power and dominion [whether angelic or human], and [far above] every name that is named [above every title that can be conferred], not only in this age and world but also in the one to come. Ephesians 1:17-21.*

AND HE CAME AND PREACHED THE GOOD NEWS OF PEACE TO YOU [Gentiles] WHO WERE FAR AWAY, AND PEACE TO THOSE [Jews] WHO WERE NEAR. For it is through Him [Christ] that we both have a [direct] way of approach in one Spirit to the Father. So then you are no longer strangers and aliens [outsiders without rights of citizenship], but you are fellow citizens with the saints (God's people), and are [members] of God's household, having been built on the foundation of the apostles and prophets, with Christ Jesus Himself as the [chief] Cornerstone, in whom the whole

*structure is joined together, and it continues [to increase] grow-
ing into a holy temple in the Lord [a sanctuary dedicated, set
apart, and sacred to the presence of the Lord]. In Him [and in
fellowship with one another] you also are being built together
into a dwelling place of God in the Spirit. Ephesians 2:17-22.*

*For this reason [grasping the greatness of this plan by which Jews
and Gentiles are joined together in Christ] I bow my knees [in
reverence] before the Father [of our Lord Jesus Christ], from
whom every family in heaven and on earth derives its name
[God—the first and ultimate Father]. May He grant you out of
the riches of His glory, to be strengthened and spiritually ener-
gized with power through His Spirit in your inner self, [indwell-
ing your innermost being and personality], so that Christ may
dwell in your hearts through your faith. And may you, having
been [deeply] rooted and [securely] grounded in love, be fully
capable of comprehending with all the saints (God's people) the
width and length and height and depth of His love [fully expe-
riencing that amazing, endless love]; and [that you may come]
to know [practically, through personal experience] the love of
Christ which far surpasses [mere] knowledge [without experi-
ence], that you may be filled up [throughout your being] to all
the fullness of God [so that you may have the richest experience
of God's presence in your lives, **completely filled and flooded
with God Himself**]. Ephesians 3:14-19.*

*Grace and peace [that special sense of spiritual well-being] be
multiplied to you in the [true, intimate] knowledge of God
and of Jesus our Lord. For His divine power has bestowed on*

THE POWERS OF THE AGE TO COME

us [absolutely] everything necessary for [a dynamic spiritual] life and godliness, through true and personal knowledge of Him who called us by His own glory and excellence. For by these He has bestowed on us His precious and magnificent promises [of inexpressible value], so that by them you may escape from the immoral freedom that is in the world because of disreputable desire, **and become sharers of the divine nature.** *For this very reason, applying your diligence [to the divine promises, make every effort] in [exercising] your faith to, develop moral excellence, and in moral excellence, knowledge (insight, understanding), and in your knowledge, self-control, and in your self-control, steadfastness, and in your steadfastness, godliness, and in your godliness, brotherly affection, and in your brotherly affection, [develop Christian] love [that is, learn to unselfishly seek the best for others and to do things for their benefit]. For as these qualities are yours and are increasing [**in you as you grow toward spiritual maturity**], they will keep you from being useless and unproductive in regard to the true knowledge and greater understanding of our Lord Jesus Christ. 2 Peter 1:2-8.*

In the Old Testament we read about outstanding miracles that God performed through Moses, Joshua, Elijah and Elisha.

Just like Elisha got a double portion of Elijah's anointing, Jesus said His followers will do greater miracles than Jesus did. Let's keep in mind that *there are also many other things which Jesus did, which if they were recorded one by one, I suppose that even the world itself could not contain the books that would be written. John 21:25.*

God's miracles through Elisha:

2 Kings 2:14 *He took the mantle of Elijah that fell from him and struck the waters and said, "Where is the Lord, the God of Elijah?" And when he also had struck the waters, they were divided here and there; and Elisha crossed over (the river).*

2 Kings 2:21-22 *He went out to the spring of water and threw salt in it and said, "Thus says the Lord, 'I have purified these waters; there shall not be from there death or unfruitfulness any longer.'" So the waters have been purified to this day, according to the word of Elisha which he spoke.*

2 Kings 2:24 *When he looked behind him and saw them, he cursed them in the name of the Lord. Then two female bears came out of the woods and tore up forty-two lads of their number.*

2 Kings 3:20 *It happened in the morning, when the sacrifice was offered, that suddenly water came [miraculously] from the area of Edom, and the country was filled with water.*

2 Kings 4:1-7 *Now a certain woman of the wives of the sons of the prophets cried out to Elisha, "Your servant my husband is dead, and you know that your servant feared the Lord; and the creditor has come to take my two children to be his slaves." Elisha said to her, "What shall I do for you? Tell me, what do you have in the house?" And she said, "Your maidservant has nothing in the house except a jar of oil." Then he said, "Go, borrow vessels at large for yourself from all your neighbors, even empty vessels; do not get a few. And you shall go in and shut the door*

behind you and your sons, and pour out into all these vessels, and you shall set aside what is full.” So she went from him and shut the door behind her and her sons; they were bringing the vessels to her and she poured. When the vessels were full, she said to her son, “Bring me another vessel.” And he said to her, “There is not one vessel more.” And the oil stopped. Then she came and told the man of God. And he said, “Go, sell the oil and pay your debt, and you and your sons can live on the rest.”

2 Kings 4:16-17 *Elisha said, “At this season next year, you will embrace a son.” She said, “No, my lord. O man of God, do not lie to your maidservant.” But the woman conceived and gave birth to a son at that season the next year, just as Elisha had said to her.*

2 Kings 4:32-35 *When Elisha came into the house, behold the lad was dead and laid on his bed. So he entered and shut the door behind them both and prayed to the Lord. And he went up and lay on the child, and put his mouth on his mouth and his eyes on his eyes and his hands on his hands, and he stretched himself on him; and the flesh of the child became warm. Then he returned and walked in the house once back and forth, and went up and stretched himself on him; and the lad sneezed seven times and the lad opened his eyes.*

2 Kings 4:38-41 *Elisha came back to Gilgal during a famine in the land. The sons of the prophets were sitting before him, and he said to his servant, “Put on the large pot and cook stew for the sons of the prophets.” Then one [of them] went into the field to gather herbs, and found a wild vine and gathered from it a*

lapful of wild gourds, and came and cut them up into the pot of stew, although they did not know what they were. So they served it for the men to eat. But as they ate the stew, they cried out, "O man of God, there is death in the pot." And they could not eat it. But he said, "Bring flour." And he threw it into the pot and said, "Serve it for the people so that they may eat." Then there was nothing harmful in the pot.

2 Kings 4:42-44 Now [at another time] a man from Baal-shalisha came and brought the man of God bread of the first fruits, twenty loaves of barley bread, and fresh ears of grain [in the husk] in his sack. And Elisha said, "Give it to the people [affected by the famine] so that they may eat." His servant said, "How am I to set [only] this before a hundred [hungry] men?" He said, "Give it to the people so that they may eat, for thus says the LORD, 'They shall eat and have some left.'" So he set it before them, and they ate and left some, in accordance with the word of the LORD.

2 Kings 5:10, 14 Elisha sent a messenger to him, saying, "Go and wash in the Jordan seven times, and your flesh will be restored to you and you will be clean."... So he went down and plunged himself into the Jordan seven times, just as the man of God had said; and his flesh was restored like that of a little child and he was clean.

2 Kings 5:25-27 Then he went in and stood before his master. Elisha asked him, "Where have you been, Gehazi?" He said, "Your servant went nowhere." Elisha said to him, "Did my heart not go with you, when the man turned from his chariot to

THE POWERS OF THE AGE TO COME   143

meet you? Is it a [proper] time to accept money and clothing and olive orchards and vineyards and sheep and oxen and male and female servants? Therefore, the leprosy of Naaman shall cling to you and to your descendants forever." So Gehazi departed from his presence, a leper as white as snow.

2 Kings 6:3-7 *Then one said, "Please be willing to go with your servants." So he answered, "I shall go." So he went with them; and when they came to the Jordan, they cut down [some of] the trees. But it happened that as one was cutting down a beam, the axe head fell into the water; and he cried out and said, "Oh no, my master! It was borrowed!" The man of God said, "Where did it fall?" When he showed him the place, Elisha cut off a stick and threw it in there, and made the iron [axe head] float. He said, "Pick it up for yourself." So he reached out with his hand and took it.*

2 Kings 6:11-14 *Now the heart of the king of Aram (Syria) was enraged over this thing. He called his servants and said to them, "Will you not tell me which of us is helping the king of Israel?" One of his servants said, "None [of us is helping him], my lord, O king; but Elisha, the prophet who is in Israel, tells the king of Israel the words that you speak in your bedroom." So he said, "Go and see where he is, so that I may send [men] and seize him." And he was told, "He is in Dothan." So he sent horses and chariots and a powerful army there. They came by night and surrounded the city.*

2 Kings 6:15-17 *The servant of the man of God got up early and went out, and behold, there was an army with horses and*

144   THROW AWAY YOUR RAPTURE RUG!

chariots encircling the city. Elisha's servant said to him, "Oh no, my master! What are we to do?" Elisha answered, "Do not be afraid, for those who are with us are more than those who are with them." Then Elisha prayed and said, "LORD, please, open his eyes that he may see." And the LORD opened the servants eyes and he saw; and behold, the mountain was full of horses and chariots of fire surrounding Elisha.

2 Kings 6:18-23 *When the Arameans came down to him, Elisha prayed to the LORD and said, "Please strike this people (nation) with blindness." And God struck them with blindness, in accordance with Elisha's request. Then Elisha said to the Arameans, "This is not the way, nor is this the city. Follow me and I will lead you to the man whom you are seeking." And he led them to Samaria. When they had come into Samaria, Elisha said, "LORD, open the eyes of these men, so that they may see." And the LORD opened their eyes and they saw. Behold, they were in the midst of Samaria. When the king of Israel (Jehoram) saw them, he said to Elisha, "My father, shall I kill them? Shall I kill them?" Elisha answered, "You shall not kill them. Would you kill those you have taken captive with your sword and bow? Serve them bread and water, so that they may eat and drink, and go back to their master [King Ben-hadad]." So the king prepared a great feast for them; and when they had eaten and drunk he sent them away, and they went to their master. And the marauding bands of Aram did not come into the land of Israel again.*

2 Kings 13:21 *As they were burying a man, behold, they saw a marauding band; and they cast the man into the grave of Elisha.*

THE POWERS OF THE AGE TO COME

And when the man touched the bones of Elisha he revived and stood up on his feet.

Incredible miracles happened in the Old Testament by the hands of God's people, under the law, under a much lesser covenant.

Under the New Covenant in Jesus' blood, the sons of God should walk in at least the same miracles that we read about in the Old covenant, and that we read that Jesus performed, as well as the apostles did in the New Testament.

Jesus came back to His disciples after He was resurrected, in a glorified body (which the sons and daughters of God will someday receive (1 Cor 15:50-54) and He was able to appear (John 20:19; Luke 24:36), vanish (Luke 24:31), eat (John 21:13; Luke 24:29-30), He still has the scars of Calvary and the holes on His side, hands and feet (Luke 24:39; John 20:26-27), His body looked different than His previous human body (John 20:14; John 21:12; Luke 24:15-16), He did many more miracles not written in the Bible (John 20:30-31).

Just as Jesus, as the Son of Man, brought to pass the will of His Father while He walked the earth, it is the will of our Father God to continue doing it through Jesus' body (the church). Even though Jesus was still divine as the Son of God, He limited Himself to completely operate as the Son of Man, to be the perfect example of what a person can accomplish when led and empowered by the Holy Spirit in intimate relationship with Father God. Jesus never misrepresented the Father, hence we must never misrepresent our heavenly Father either.

There will be a generation that will understand that the sons of God are not mere humans but truly new creatures, that carry such presence of God that the creation around them will find relief from the sin and evil that hinders and keeps it in bondage. When God created the garden in Eden, He expected Adam, Eve and their descendants to transform the whole earth to look like it. The garden was their starting point, where they were learning, God was going to help them do it, but they missed it and instead everything was cursed. Jesus broke the curse for those who believe in Him, He has given them authority and power to carry out God's original design and intent for the earth that Adam could not accomplish. He still wants to help us do it and has provided everything we will ever need to do it. From the beginning our good Father God has desired to partner with mankind through divine intervention to subdue the earth and to make it a beautiful and perfect shadow of heaven. Some may say that it will be in the millennium, if that was true, why then is the body of Christ still on the earth? Why not just get saved and right after go to heaven? But that's not what the Bible says about the will of God.

Revelation 5:9-10 says:

And they sang a new song [of glorious redemption], saying,

"Worthy and deserving are You to take the scroll and to break its seals; for You were slain (sacrificed), and with Your blood You purchased people for God from every tribe and language and people and nation. "You have made them to be a kingdom [of royal subjects] and priests to our God; **and they will reign on the earth."**

IF Salvation became available after Jesus rose from the dead and presented His blood on heaven's mercy seat in God's throne room (Dan 7:13-14; Heb 9:24-25). His blood purchased salvation for all the people who chose to believe and accept Him as Father God's only begotten Son, becoming through obedience to God the perfect eternal sacrifice for the redemption of human souls and the reconciliation of mankind to Father God, from Adam and Eve (Eph 4:8-9; 1 Pet 4:6) to the last person that will be born on the earth, THEN ruling and reigning with Him as His body ought to be during the same period of time which is NOW.

Isaiah 65:17-24 talks about a new heaven and a new earth where people will live over one hundred years old, they will work, they will reproduce, there will be vegetation, etc. This has to be on earth, before the earth will be actually destroyed because when that day comes, there will be no death.

"Behold, I am creating new heavens and a new earth; And the former things [of life] will not be remembered or come to mind. "But be glad and rejoice forever over what I create; Behold, I am creating Jerusalem to be a source of rejoicing And her people a joy. "I will also rejoice in Jerusalem and be glad in My people;

And there will no longer be heard in her The voice of weeping and the sound of crying. "No longer shall there be in it an infant who lives only a few days, Or an old man who does not finish his days; For the youth who dies at the age of a hundred, And the one who does not reach the age of a hundred will be thought of as accursed. "They will build houses and live in them; They will plant vineyards and eat the fruit. "They will not build and another occupy; They will not plant and another eat [the fruit]. For as the lifetime of a tree, so will be the days of My people, And My chosen [people] will fully enjoy [and long make use of] the work of their hands. "They will not labor in vain, Or bear children for disaster; For they are the descendants of those blessed by the LORD, And their offspring with them. "It shall also come to pass that before they call, I will answer; and while they are still speaking, I will hear.

Psalm 110:2 says *The LORD will send the scepter of Your strength from Zion, saying, "Rule in the midst of Your enemies."* There are no enemies in heaven, and there will not be enemies in the Millennium. Ruling and reigning for the body of Christ is NOW.

The apostle Paul reveals in Ephesians 1:9-10:

*He made known to us the mystery of His will according to His good pleasure, which He purposed in Christ, with regard to the fulfillment of the times [that is, the end of history, the climax of the ages]—**to bring all things together in Christ, [both] things in the heavens and things on the earth.***

The body of Jesus Christ will need to walk in the powers of the age to come as the last of the last days gets closer. The church will need to experience them, more than to only know about them, to survive the times we are entering in.

As to 2022 much of the "body of Christ" is carnally minded, spiritually infant, quoting scriptures out of soulish emotional state, powerless and has greatly misrepresented God. On 2019 and 2020 there should have been the greatest healing movement in the history of mankind, but the body of Christ as a whole hid behind closed doors, and allowed all the evil outlets flood their souls with fear and unbelief. This time was meant to end Pentecost or the church age and to move into the Kingdom Age, but the church didn't move. It chose to stay in the wilderness, like the people out of Egypt. They were fed, protected, provided for, and were afraid to face the giants in the promised land. In a comparative way, many many Christians all around the world chose to stay in the comfort of their houses, with their masks, phones, "christian tv", food, toilet paper... They even chose to stay there after all had passed. Many already died in the wilderness, killed by a plague while having Jehovah Rapha in their hearts. Only the faithful remnant got in the secret place with God, got their strength and their instructions, then got out, put out tent revivals and the signs and miracles still are following their preaching of the gospel of salvation. Only the faithful remnant here and there took it as the opportunity it was to show how loving and powerful our God is. They fed the hungry, clothed the naked, helped the needy... The christian church failed the test and will die in the wilderness. The greatest harvest of all times will have to wait a little longer because the church doesn't have the capability to disciple the billions of people that are coming into God's kingdom. The faithful remnant has to get ready to harvest souls, to disciple them and to lead the reformation in the nations of the world.

The powers of the age to come are needed to multiply food, heal the waters, heal the food, heal the land and all that is in it. They are needed to part the waters, to know what the evil rulers are plotting and to warn kings about it, to thwart those evil plans. The wealth of the wicked will be transferred to the righteous ones, those who have and will pass the test of money.

The believers that will taste the powers of the age to come will be those who will answer the prayer "Your kingdom come Your will be done on earth as it is in heaven". They will bring the transition from the church age to the Kingdom of God age. The nations have to be discipled, the will of God has to be fulfilled. God wins. The believers in Christ win. Jesus' victory over hell and death has to be more than printed words, more than spiritual victory. It has to be shown in the natural. Jesus gave His body (the church) all the power and all the authority over all the power of the enemy; this has to be a visible reality in the natural.

As of 2022, the "body of Christ" as a whole is weak, fearful, doubtful, sick, powerless, bound, naked, poor, ignorant, etc. The idea of Jesus return to rescue His bride now would portray a complete failure of God's plan, purpose and victory over His enemies. The evil one has overplayed his cards to stop the move of God among His faithful remnant, trying to stop the harvest of a billion souls. God will pour out His Spirit over all flesh, His glory will shine more brilliant and glorious at the time of utmost darkness. His people will arise and shine in victory, in power and authority, in wisdom and understanding, walking with God in such a way that the gates of hell will not prevail against them, ushering the new era on the earth. God will see His word come to pass. Then the evil one will have his three and a half years of unrestrained evil. Then, the Millennium!!

There's much more to be said about this but only few can endure it.

Until this Word of God is fulfilled, Jesus can not come back.

CHAPTER 11

POSSESSING THE LAND AND THE FEAST OF TABERNACLES

When the people of Israel came out from Egypt under Moses leadership, the Lord commanded them to celebrate the Feasts of the Lord.

* The people of Israel and Moses celebrated the 1st Passover right before their deliverance out of Egypt and the Feast of Unleavened Bread	Exo 12
Celebration of the Feast of Passover	Lev 23
Jesus was sacrificed on the Feast of Passover becoming the Lamb of God that takes away the sins of the world. Through His sacrifice for Salvation, mankind comes out of the World (Egypt) into God's eternal kingdom.	Matt 27; John 1:29

* The people of Israel and the conse-cration of the first born	Exo 13
Jesus became the First born from the dead	Col 1:13-20
* The Lord provided mana (bread from heaven) for Israel in the desert for 40 years	Exo 16:4-5, 14-19, 31-35
Jesus is the bread of life and the bread from heaven	John 6:35, 48-51 1 Cor 10:15-16
* The Lord provided meat for Israel in the desert	Exo 16:13
Jesus' flesh is the meat from heaven	John 6:52-57
* The Lord provided water from the rock for Israel in the desert	Exo 17:5-6; Num 20:9-11
Jesus is the rock	1 Cor 10:1-4;
Jesus gives living water	John 4:14
* The Lord performed miraculous healings in the wilderness	Num 16:46-48; Num 21:9
Jesus healed all who were sick	Matt 4:23; Luke 4:40
* The Lord was with Israel in the cloud and the pillar of fire	Exo 13:21-22
The Lord lives inside every believer in Jesus Christ	Rom 8:11
* The Feast of First Fruits	Lev 23:9-14

Jesus resurrection	1 Cor 15:20-24
* The Feast of Weeks or Ingathering (Pentecost)	Lev 23:15-22
First ever baptism in the Holy Spirit and fire at Pentecost, beginning of the Harvest of souls	John 1:32; Acts 2; Luke 10:2

In the Bible we find patterns, stories, history, shadows, and prophetic descriptions (foreshadows). Ecclesiastes 1:19 says *That which has been is that which will be [again], And that which has been done is that which will be done again. So there is nothing new under the sun.*

Interpreting the times by the Holy Spirit allows the body of Christ to know where we are at and what to do about it. The apostle Paul explains this in Colossians 2:16-17 *Therefore let no one judge you in regard to food and drink or in regard to [the observance of] a festival or a new moon or a Sabbath day. Such things are only a shadow of what is to come and they have only symbolic value; but the substance [the reality of what is foreshadowed] belongs to Christ.*

Even though God had promised Abraham that his descendants would inherit certain land in the future, when the time came, the Israelites didn't just walked over and everything was ready for them. They had to war with the people living there.

Note that most of the people who came out of Egypt didn't cross over because of their fear (not to trust God) and unbelief. Heb 3:19.

After 40 years in the desert, the Israelites crossed the Jordan river to possess the promised land. In the sight of the Holy God of heaven and earth, the inhabitants of the land were idolatrous and evil. We read in Genesis 15:16 that God told Abraham: *Then in the fourth generation your descendants shall return here [to Canaan, the land of promise], for the wickedness and guilt of the Amorites is not yet complete (finished)."* The nations living in the promised land, many of them were nations of giants (a hybrid race), had heard about the great power of the God of Israel but they continued worshiping their lesser gods or idols doing things that are abomination to God.

The Israelites had to fight to possess the promised land. First they had to fight fear and unbelief in their God, then they had to physically go to war. God was with them and gave them the victory as long as they remained faithful to the Lord, and they had to observe the ways of the Lord to maintain or keep the land and to be blessed. The Lord gave them specific instructions about what to do with/to the former inhabitants in the promised land.

In Exodus 23:20-33 we read what He expected Israel (His people) to do, and He said how it would be done.

I will not drive them out before you in a single year, so that the land does not become desolate [due to lack of attention] and the [wild] animals of the field do not become too numerous for you. I will drive them out before you little by little, until you have increased and are strong enough to take possession of the land. Exo 23:29-30.

The Feast of Weeks or Pentecost was at the beginning and end of the harvest. Jesus told His disciples the harvest was ready and abundant: *Now after this the Lord appointed seventy others, and sent them out ahead of Him, two by two, into every city and place where He was about to go. He was saying to them, "The harvest is abundant [for there are many who need to hear the good news about salvation], but the workers [those available to proclaim the message of salvation] are few. Therefore, [prayerfully] ask the Lord of the harvest to send out workers into His harvest. Luke 10:1-2.*

Right before Jesus ascended to heaven, He instructed His disciples to wait for the Holy Spirit because they would need Him to accomplish the Great Commission to preach the good news of salvation and to teach or disciple all the nations about the kingdom of God. (Matt 28:16-20; Acts 1:8).

Right after the baptism of the Holy Spirit in the upper room, the harvest of souls started with 3,000 people as we read in Acts 2:41-43 *So then, those who accepted his message were baptized; and on that day about 3,000 souls were added [to the body of believers]. They were continually and faithfully devoting themselves to the instruction of the apostles, and to fellowship, to eating meals together and to prayers. A sense of awe was felt by everyone, and many wonders and signs (attesting miracles) were taking place through the apostles.*

We still are in The Harvest that Jesus talked about. The body of Christ has not completed the job to preach the gospel of salvation to all the corners of the earth, neither has fulfilled the commission to disciple the nations of the world about the gospel of the Kingdom. We're not only to pray *Your kingdom come, your will be done on earth as it is in heaven (Matt 6:10)* but it is through Jesus' Body that the will of God will be done on the earth. The body of Christ, as a whole, has not experienced the Baptism of Holy Spirit and Fire in the same way the first apostles did. We're lacking the many wonders and signs (attesting miracles) that FOLLOW the preaching of the gospels.

This takes us to the crossing of the Jordan river under Joshua's leadership. Joshua is a figure of Jesus.

Now it happened after the death of Moses the servant of the LORD, that the LORD spoke to Joshua the son of Nun, Moses' servant (attendant), saying, "Moses My servant is dead; now therefore arise [to take his place], cross over this Jordan, you and all this people, into the land which I am giving to them, to the sons of Israel. I have given you every place on which the sole of your foot treads, just as I promised to Moses. From the wilderness [of Arabia in the south] and this Lebanon [in the north], even as far as the great river, the river Euphrates [in the east], all the land of the Hittites (Canaan), and as far as the Great [Mediterranean] Sea toward the west shall be your territory. No man will [be able to] stand before you [to oppose you] as long as you live. Just as I was [present] with Moses, so will I be with you; I will not fail you or abandon you. Be strong and confident and courageous, for you will give this people as an inheritance the land which I swore to their fathers (ancestors) to give them. Only be strong and very courageous; be careful to do [everything] in accordance with the entire law which Moses My servant commanded you; do not turn from it to the right or to the left, so that you may prosper and be successful wherever you go. This Book of the Law shall not depart from your mouth, but you shall read [and meditate on] it day and night, so that you may be careful to do [everything] in accordance with all that is written in it; for then you will make your way prosperous, and then you will be successful. Have I not commanded you? Be strong and courageous! Do not be terrified or dismayed (intimidated), for the LORD your God is with you wherever you go." Joshua 1:1-9.

Just like Joshua brought the remnant of Israel to the promised land, Jesus took the captivity captive and translated them to paradise in heaven (Eph 4:8) and became the way into the promise land (God's kingdom) by His blood to reconcile mankind to Father God (2 Cor 5:17-19).

In Joshua's farewell address (Josh 23), he gives Israel instructions of how to keep the land and to be blessed by the Lord. Jesus gave the same instructions and so did the apostles. They all talked about a place of rest where God will fight our battles, but they all are connected to believe and trust in God.

With Joshua, the promised land was the physical land where the presence of the Lord could be seen and heard. God was with them in the Tent of Meeting, and they could literally see His wonderful acts every time they obeyed His instructions and remained in His ways.

With Jesus, the promised land was the spiritual heavenly Paradise in God's kingdom. God Almighty is in the real tabernacle or Throne Room in heaven, where Jesus sprinkled His own blood on the mercy seat.

Jesus finished complete work went far beyond salvation, and reconciliation between Father God and humankind: it made possible to bring together the physical and the spiritual, heaven and earth together: *and through [the intervention of] the Son to reconcile all things to Himself, making peace [with believers] through the blood of His cross; through Him, [I say,] whether things on earth or things in heaven. Col 1:20.*

The hearts of the body of Christ are the promised land, God has made their spirits His place of dwelling or the Holy of Holies. The believer must strive and work to enter in God's rest which is in the secret place of the Most High.

Therefore, while the promise of entering His rest still remains and is freely offered today, let us fear, in case any one of you may seem to come short of reaching it or think he has come too late. For indeed we have had the good news [of salvation] preached to us, just as the Israelites also [when the good news of the promised land came to them]; but the message they heard did not benefit them, because it was not united with faith [in God] by those who heard. For we who believe [that is, we who personally trust and confidently rely on God] enter that rest [so we have His inner peace now because we are confident in our salvation, and assured of His power], just as He has said,

"As I swore [an oath] in My wrath, They shall not enter My rest,"

[this He said] although His works were completed from the foundation of the world [waiting for all who would believe].

For somewhere [in Scripture] He has said this about the seventh day: "And God rested on the seventh day from all His works"; and again in this, "They shall not enter My rest." Therefore, since the promise remains for some to enter His rest, and those who formerly had the good news preached to them failed to [grasp it and did not] enter because of [their unbelief evidenced by] disobedience, He again sets a definite day, [a new] "Today," [providing another opportunity to enter that rest by] saying through David after so long a time, just as has been said before [in the words already quoted],

"Today if you hear His voice, Do not harden your hearts."

[This mention of a rest was not a reference to their entering into Canaan.] For if Joshua had given them rest, God would not speak about another day [of opportunity] after that. So there remains a [full and complete] Sabbath rest for the people of God. For the one who has once entered His rest has also rested from [the weariness and pain of] his [human] labors, just as God rested from [those labors uniquely] His own. Let us therefore make every effort to enter that rest [of God, to know and experience

it for ourselves], so that no one will fall by following the same example of disobedience [as those who died in the wilderness]. Hebrews 4:1-11.

There still is another time for this rest, which will be the Millennium, the seventh day.

In a couple parables of the money usage we read what Jesus expects from His body (Luke 19:1-27 and Matthew 25:14-30).

While they were listening to these things, Jesus went on to tell a parable, because He was near Jerusalem, and they assumed that the kingdom of God was going to appear immediately [as soon as He reached the city]. So He said, "A nobleman went to a distant country to obtain for himself a kingdom, and [then] to return. So he called ten of his servants, and gave them ten minas [one apiece, each equal to about a hundred days' wages] and said to them, 'Do business [with this] until I return.' But his citizens [the residents of his new kingdom] hated him and sent a delegation after him, saying, 'We do not want this man to be a king over us.' When he returned, after receiving the kingdom, he ordered that these servants, to whom he had given the money, be called to him, that he might find out what business they had done. The first one came before him and said, 'Lord, your mina has made ten more minas.' And he said to him, 'Well done, good servant! **Because you proved yourself faithful and trustworthy in a very little thing, you shall [now] have authority over ten cities** *[in my kingdom].' The second one came and said, 'Lord, your mina has made five minas.' And he said to him also, '**And you shall take charge over five cities.**' Then* *another came and said, 'Lord, here is your mina, which I have kept laid up in a handkerchief [for safekeeping]. I was [always] afraid of you, because you are a stern man; you pick up what you did not lay down and you reap what you did not sow.' He said to the servant, 'I will judge and condemn you by your own words, you worthless servant! Did you [really] know that I was a stern man, picking up what I did not lay down and reaping what I did not sow? Then why did you not [at the very least] put my money in a bank? Then on my return, I would have collected it with interest.' Then he said to the bystanders, 'Take the mina away from him and give it to the one who has the ten minas.' And they said to him, 'Lord, he has ten minas already!' [Jesus explained,] 'I tell you that to everyone who has [because he valued his gifts from God and has used them wisely], more will be given; but from the one who does not have [because he disregarded his gifts from God], even what he has will be taken away.' [The king ended by saying,] 'But as for these enemies of mine who did not want me to be king over them, bring them here and kill them in my presence.'" Luke 19:1-27.*

Jesus gives of His own estate and resources to those of His house, He expects His people to multiply the resources received and to give them back to the Lord. Jesus will give it all back to the faithful ones but notice the parable says the Lord also gives them authority over cities.

Just like God was with Joshua and the people of Israel after they crossed the Jordan river, Jesus provided and made available for His people everything they will need to possess the earth, starting with the same power that raised Jesus from the dead (His Holy Spirit) living inside the believers in Christ Jesus.

Ephesians 1:18-23 explains all this and makes clear that the evil one does not have any authority anymore over the earth and over mankind.

And [I pray] that the eyes of your heart [the very center and core of your being] may be enlightened [flooded with light by the Holy Spirit], so that you will know and cherish the hope [the divine guarantee, the confident expectation] to which He has called you, the riches of His glorious inheritance in the saints (God's people), and [so that you will begin to know] what the immeasurable and unlimited and surpassing greatness of His [active, spiritual] power is in us who believe. These are in accordance with the working of His mighty strength which He produced in Christ when He raised Him from the dead and seated Him at His own right hand in the heavenly places, far above all rule and authority and power and dominion [whether angelic or human], and [far above] every name that is named [above every title that can be conferred], not only in this age and world but also in the one to come. And He (Father God) put all things [in every realm] in subjection under Christ's feet, and appointed Him as [supreme and authoritative] head over all things in the church, which is His body, the fullness of Him who fills and completes all things in all [believers].

Just like Joshua took the promised land with supernatural help, being obedient to every instruction God gave him; the body of Christ must take the land that the evil one has illegally kept, and do the will of God on that land as it is in heaven.

Psalm 2:8 says *Ask of Me, and I will assuredly give [You] the nations as Your inheritance, And the ends of the earth as Your possession.* This has to be done through Jesus' body (the church).

Jesus' disciples expected Jesus to establish His kingdom on the earth and to deliver them from the bondage of Rome. They expected Him to become their King and they expected to rule side by side with Him *(Then [Salome] the mother of Zebedee's children [James and John] came up to Jesus with her sons and, kneeling down [in respect], asked a favor of Him. And He said to her, "What do you wish?" She answered Him, "Command that in Your kingdom these two sons of mine may sit [in positions of honor and authority] one on Your right and one on Your left." Matt 20:20-21.)* They didn't understand Jesus purpose on earth at that time.

Then the disciples were baptized with Holy Spirit and Fire and they became preachers of the good news of salvation, miracles, signs and wonders followed them, they discipled people and gave their lives to their calling. Even though the christian churches were multiplying, they fell short of understanding that the way the kingdom of God will be established on the earth is through the body of Jesus (the church) and not through a sovereign move of God as it was in creation. Jesus as the Head, the King of Kings, and the church as His body doing the work.

Slowly the church encamped around the message that "Jesus is coming back", "Jesus is coming soon", and instead of discipleing the nations and instead of "Your kingdom come Your will be done on earth as it is in heaven", they started selling all their possessions, distributing their goods and money among the believers (Acts 2:44-47) and expecting the rapture at any time. It got so bad that the apostle Paul had to give them instructions in 2 Thess 3:10-12 *For even while we were with you, we used to give you this order: if anyone is not willing to work, then he is not to eat, either. Indeed, we hear that some among you are leading an undisciplined and inappropriate life, doing no work at all, but acting like busybodies [meddling in other people's business]. Now such people we command and exhort in the Lord Jesus Christ to settle down and work quietly and earn their own food and other necessities [supporting themselves instead of depending on the hospitality of others].*

As to 2022, the American christian church as a whole has done a good job investing in the spreading of the gospel of salvation into all the earth, but has also fallen short of understanding the importance of reformation, and she is waiting for the rapture to rescue her from the darkness that is spreading around, instead of being the restrainer, city on a hill, light in the darkness, salt of the earth, that God expects the whole christian church to be.

The judgment we read about in Matthew 25:31-46 deals with the nations of the earth. The sheep and the goat nations, *"But when the Son of Man comes in His glory and majesty and all the angels with Him, then He will sit on the throne of His glory.* **All the nations will be gathered** *before Him [for judgment]; and He will separate them from one another, as a shepherd separates his sheep from the goats; and He will put the sheep on His right [the place of honor], and the goats on His left [the place of rejection]. (verses 31-33).*

Remember Jesus was a Jew so when He said in Matthew 25:38-40 *And when did we see You as a stranger, and invite You in, or naked, and clothe You? And when did we see You sick, or in prison, and come to You?' The King will answer and say to them, 'I assure you and most solemnly say to you,* **to the extent that you did it for one of these brothers of Mine**, *even the least of them, you did it for Me.'* Jesus was talking about the nation of Israel, the Jews are His brothers. The sheep nations are the ones that help Israel. The goat nations are the ones who despise Israel and do her evil. *"Then He will say to those on His left, 'Leave Me, you cursed ones, into the eternal fire which has been prepared for the devil and his angels (demons); for I was hungry, and you gave Me nothing to eat; I was thirsty, and you gave Me nothing to drink; I was a stranger, and you did not invite Me in; naked, and you did not clothe Me; sick, and in prison, and you did not visit Me [with help and ministering care].' Then they also [in their turn] will answer, 'Lord, when did we see You hungry, or thirsty, or as a stranger, or naked, or sick, or in prison, and did not minister to You?' Then He will reply to them, 'I assure you and most solemnly say to you, to the extent that you did not do it for one of the least of these [my followers], you did not do it for Me.' (verses 41-45).*

God promised Abraham in Genesis 12:1-3 *Now [in Haran] the* LORD *had said to Abram, "Go away from your country, And from your relatives And from your father's house, To the land which I will show you;* ***And I will make you a great nation****, And I will bless you [abundantly], And make your name great (exalted, distinguished); And you shall be a blessing [a source of great good to others]; And I will bless (do good for, benefit) those who bless you, And I will curse [that is, subject to My wrath and judgment] the one who curses (despises, dishonors, has contempt for) you.* ***And in you all the families (nations) of the earth will be blessed.****"*

When Israel finally possessed the promised land, every part of life was subject to the ways of the Lord. They had the law of Moses and commandments to follow which were the guarantee of God's protection and blessings. The nations around them feared them because of their God.

So the LORD *gave Israel all the land which He had sworn to give to their fathers (ancestors), and they took possession of it and lived in it. The* LORD *gave them rest [from conflict] on every side, in accordance with everything that He had sworn to their fathers, and not one of all their enemies stood before them [in battle]; the* LORD *handed over all their enemies to them. Not one of the good promises which the* LORD *had spoken to the house of Israel failed; all had come to pass. Joshua 21:43-45.*

Every part of the nation of Israel's life was subject to God's ways. For instance: *that Joshua called all Israel,* ***their elders and their heads and their judges and their officers****, and said to them, Josh 23:2.*

168   THROW AWAY YOUR RAPTURE RUG!

Now days the areas of social life are called Mountains, Spheres or Gates. God gave His modern prophets understanding that Christianity was never meant to be a religion but a way of life influencing Arts & Entertainment, Business, Education, Family, Government, Media, and Religion.

Proverbs 29:2 says *When the righteous are in authority and become great, the people rejoice; But when the wicked man rules, the people groan and sigh. (Read the whole chapter).*

We have seen first hand how bad things can get because the body of Christ refused to take over, and have allowed un-redeemed ones dictate everything in society. Up to 2022 every sphere of society is bent to evil calling good evil and evil good, rejecting everything that mentions the name of Jesus and despising the ways of the Lord. Lawlessness and murderer are celebrated, and true justice is hardly ever seen. The murderer of unborn children has been made law and millions of dollars are poured out into that abomination. There's a faithful remnant working against these giants, but the calling is for the whole body of Christ to raise up and to take over. It is the goodness of God that leads people to repentance (Rom 2:4), the goodness of God has to be seen in every part of social life, righteousness and justice, holiness and purity must prevail in every sphere of society.

The body of Christ must reign the earth with an iron scepter and not allow evil get away with anything, the gates of hell shall not prevail against the Christian church (Matt 16:18).

Isaiah 9:6a says *For to us a Child shall be born, to us a Son shall be given; And the **government shall be upon His shoulder.*** Colossians 1:18 says *He (Christ) is also the head [the life-source and leader] of the body, the church;* Jesus is the head, the church is the body that does what the head commands. It is the responsibility of the body of Christ to possess the land and to occupy every sphere of society to make it operate as it is in heaven.

That's the reason why Jesus commanded to *disciple the nations.* The great evangelistic campaigns/crusades are awesome, millions of people hear the gospel of salvation and are drawn to Jesus, BUT the body of Christ has greatly failed to make disciples and teaching people the Gospel of the Kingdom, the way life is in the Kingdom of God, on earth as it is in heaven. Revival and Awakening are the means God uses for a massive harvest of souls, the Holy Spirit moves in powerful new ways that cause conviction of sins and the realization of the need of a personal savior. Then comes Discipleship, where people learn how to have a relationship with the LORD, how to hear the voice of God, how to know God and to know their destiny, how to draw near to Him and walk with Him in holiness and purity, how to become soldiers of the cross, how to be led by the person Holy Spirit, and the ways of the Kingdom of God and how to walk in the powers of the age to come. Then Reformation is what transforms culture and society on earth as it is in heaven.

Unlike Joshua and the people of Israel that through physical war annihilated or displaced the nations that were in the promised land, the new covenant in the blood of Christ made a different way to possess the earth: Jesus reconciles people with Father God so that they have direct access to God's throne of grace to establish not only their identity in Him, but to get the spirit of wisdom and understanding in the knowledge of Him, to learn how the kingdom of heaven operates, and the strategies, witty ideas and inventions to take over every area of life. We disciple nations by love going to war in the spirit, binding the spiritual strong man, and operating in the supernatural ways of God.

The church has done "spiritual warfare" year after year, mega churches are in every major city, yet there has not been any impact in actually taking the cities for Jesus. His government is not established, all spheres of social life are not subject to the King of Majesty. Then, the evil one comes back to where he was and finds the city clean and empty of righteous authority and comes with seven evil spirits more wicked than him and makes the city worse than it was before.

The ministry of reconciliation the apostle Paul talks about in 2 Corinthians 5:18 *But all these things are from God, who reconciled us to Himself through Christ [making us acceptable to Him] and gave us the ministry of reconciliation [so that by our example we might bring others to Him], that is, that God was in Christ reconciling the world to Himself, not counting people's sins against them [but canceling them]. And He has committed to us the message of reconciliation [that is, restoration to favor with God].* By the blood of Christ Jesus we are reconciled to

God our Father. In like manner parents and children will be reconciled by repentance in a bond of love. As of 2022 the evil seeds planted for the last 40 years to poison the children's minds, to break families and the bond of love between children and their parents and grand parents has produced a harvest of rebellion and witchcraft around the world. But there's a promise that has not been fulfilled yet:

Through Malachi 4:5-6, the Lord says: *"Behold, I am going to send you Elijah the prophet before the coming of the great and terrible day of the LORD. He will turn the hearts of the fathers to their children, and the hearts of the children to their fathers [a reconciliation produced by repentance], so that I will not come and strike the land with a curse [of complete destruction]."*

The evil one has worked over time to discredit and diminish parental figures, and separating families. This dismemberment of the family has caused the land to become cursed. Because of this separation among the family members, the children have no protection against all kinds of evil spirits and human predators.

The reconciliation between parents and their children has to happen before the second coming of Jesus.

Reformation is done by all the members of the body of Christ taking their places in the areas of society where God has placed them, being led by the Holy Spirit, using their God given practical and spiritual gifts, and following the recommendations of the apostles' letters in the New Testament of the Bible. Jesus and the leaders of the church in the times of the first apostles spent long times in the presence of God, in worship, prayer, and reading and meditating (thinking about) God's word. No only allowing Father God to love them but receiving everyday instructions.

The apostle Paul said we must pray at all times. *With all prayer and petition pray [with specific requests] at all times [on every occasion and in every season] in the Spirit, and with this in view, stay alert with all perseverance and petition [interceding in prayer] for all God's people. And pray for me, that words may be given to me when I open my mouth, to proclaim boldly the mystery of the good news [of salvation], for which I am an ambassador in chains. And pray that in proclaiming it I may speak boldly and courageously, as I should. Ephesians 6:18-20.*

I thank God that I speak in [unknown] tongues more than all of you; 1 Cor 14:18

It was during those times with Father God that Jesus saw what His Father was doing and heard what Father God was saying:

So Jesus answered them by saying, "I assure you and most solemnly say to you, the Son can do nothing of Himself [of His own accord], unless it is something He sees the Father doing; for whatever things the Father does, the Son [in His turn] also does in the same way. For the Father dearly loves the Son and shows Him everything that He Himself is doing; and the Father will show Him greater works than these, so that you will be filled with wonder. John 5:19-20.

For I have never spoken on My own initiative or authority, but the Father Himself who sent Me has given Me a commandment regarding what to say and what to speak. I know that His commandment is eternal life. So the things I speak, I speak [in accordance with His exact instruction,] just as the Father has told Me." John 12:49-50.

Reformation will only happen when the body of Christ understands its need to stay attached to Jesus (the head of the body), and spends time in the presence of Father God. We don't have to wait until we are perfected in our hearing and seeing what our Father God is doing and saying, but we must diligently ask the Holy Spirit for help, wisdom, understanding, faith, counsel etc., and obey Him when He tells us something.

For instance, teachers can privately pray for every one of his/her students, lay hands on their chairs and desks before they get in the classroom releasing the anointing and declaring blessings, and continually pray (quietly) in the spirit at his/her desk and chair until it's saturated with the anointing of God. As they carry God's presence and goodness, the students will be drawn to them asking why they feel so safe and at peace in that classroom. The teacher doesn't have to carry the Bible around and be preachy, Holy Spirit will speak to their hearts, when they ask then the door will be open to tell them about Jesus and the love of Father God.

In Acts 6:1-6 we read that the apostles chose seven men to serve tables and distribute food in the congregation: *"It is not appropriate for us to neglect [teaching] the word of God in order to serve tables and manage the distribution of food. Therefore, brothers, choose from among you seven **men with good reputations [men of godly character and moral integrity], full of the Spirit and of wisdom,** whom we may put in charge of this task... The suggestion pleased the whole congregation; and they selected **Stephen, a man full of faith [in Christ Jesus], and [filled with and led by] the Holy Spirit, and Philip...***

Notice the requirements to be chosen "to serve tables and to manage the distribution of food". In Acts 8:4-6 we read how God confirmed the gospel Philip was preaching with signs, miracles and wonders.

No matter where the believers in Christ are, that place is their mission field, God has placed them there to harvest those souls and to claim that land for King Jesus. Wherever you are, get to your work place early and pray over the furniture and release God's anointing in the name of Jesus, release God's peace, pray frequently for your co workers, clients, boss, etc. release God's anointing in the food you serve, in the packages you deliver, be attentive to the people around you, be led by the Holy Spirit and be ready to pray for them. Plead the blood of Christ over that piece of property, break every curse over the land and claim it for King Jesus. If you own the place of business, anoint it with oil, plead the blood of Christ over it and declare your place is holy ground.

Train your tongue to not curse that place or people. Stop declaring how much you hate this or that. God placed you there to be a blessing, a delight, to show the world how the children of the Most High God are **men and women with good reputations [of godly character and moral integrity], full of the Spirit and of wisdom.** It is the goodness of God that leads to repentance. That place where you are at is where you must war with the spiritual authority and the spiritual weapons (2 Cor 10:4) Jesus has given you. That's how God's sons and daughters will take and posses the land. Not by preaching, condemning, and criticizing but by good example, godly character, moral integrity, full of the Holy Spirit and wisdom, executing justice and in righteousness, and full of joy.

Every person has God given gifts meant to be a blessing and to influence his/her environment. Practical gifts like painting, singing, dancing, understanding technology, creating, cooking, designing, training, building, etc. Sometimes the Lord requires His children to set aside their own dreams and plans to do Father God's will, but God always rewards those who are obedient and who put God's will first over their own. It is in this kind of total abandonment to the will of God that in due time Father God gives them the desires of their hearts exceedingly, abundantly, above and beyond their sanctified wildest dreams and desires.

The Feast of Harvest or Pentecost foreshadowed the harvest of human souls by the blood of Jesus through the gospel of salvation, but it was not and is not meant to last forever. Billions of people will enter God's kingdom. In the end there will be much more people in Paradise than in hell.

When the King of Glory sits on His throne in the city of David (Bethel) during the Millennium, He is going to rule over every facet of life with a rod of iron. Sin will not be allowed. At that time, after the wrath of God has been poured out to completely destroy all the wicked people and wicked cities of the earth, and the nations have been dealt with as sheep and goat nations. Then King Jesus will start rebuilding the earth with His holy ones in their glorified bodies, and everything will be under His rule. People will still have the freedom to chose, but there will be consequences to disobedience.

No one knows the day or the hour (Matt 24:26) **but we are not unaware** (1 Thes 5:4).

The Messianic prophecies and the Spring Feasts of the Lord foretold and foreshadowed the first coming of Messiah.

The Millennial prophecies and the Fall Feasts of The Lord foretell and foreshadow the second coming of Christ.

To fulfill the next Feast after Pentecost, The Feast of Trumpets (Lev 23:23-25) which foreshadows The Second coming of the Lord (in 1 Cor 15:50-58 the apostle Paul states "at the last trumpet"), we must first complete the assignment to bring in the whole harvest and to possess the land, the nations as the inheritance of Jesus. Remember, the evil one should only be allowed three and a half years to do what he wants, after the Holy Spirit and the body of Christ – the restrainers- are taken out of the earth.

The apostle Paul says it will be "at the last trumpet" (1 Cor 15:51-52). We don't know at what Feast of Trumpets, nor the day or the hour because the Jewish calendar is quite different from the world's calendar, but we know it will be in the fall. No one knows the day or the hour when Father will send Jesus back to earth, only Father God knows. Let's just make sure when Christ returns He will find faith on the earth, and that we will be ready for Him at all times.

Right now the earth is travailing like birth pangs, and it is very upset because of the sinful actions of mankind. In Psalms and Revelation we read what will happen to the earth when the wrath of God will be released, which will also release all the energy stored underground through earthquakes and volcanic eruptions but Christ's body is not appointed to God's wrath.

The Feast of Tabernacles speaks about the Millenium where the earth will rest just as God rested in the seventh day of creation. God will dwell or tabernacle with mankind and the saints in their glorified bodies will rule with Him. We also read that there will be one thousand years of rebuilding and great peace and harmony. One thousand years where the Lord Jesus will rule with a scepter of iron, He will not allow sin on the earth just like there is no sin in the kingdom of heaven. The whole earth will finally look like the garden in Eden. The apostle Peter explains some of these things in 2 Peter 3.

Also Father God will not send Jesus back to earth until all His enemies become His footstool. *'THE LORD (the Father) SAID TO MY LORD (the Son, the Messiah), "SIT AT MY RIGHT HAND, UNTIL I MAKE YOUR ENEMIES A FOOTSTOOL FOR YOUR FEET."' Luke 20:42b-43.*

Hebrews 10:11-13 says: *Every priest stands [at his altar of service] ministering daily, offering the same sacrifices over and over, which are never able to strip away sins [that envelop and cover us]; whereas Christ, having offered the one sacrifice [the all-sufficient sacrifice of Himself] for sins for all time, SAT DOWN [signifying the completion of atonement for sin] AT THE RIGHT HAND OF GOD [the position of honor], waiting from that time onward UNTIL HIS ENEMIES ARE MADE A FOOTSTOOL FOR HIS FEET.*

There's another thing that has to be fulfilled before the Lord Jesus returns, but just as the full number of the gentiles the number of the martyrs will remain unknown to us:

When He (the Lamb) broke open the fifth seal, I saw underneath the altar the souls of those who had been slaughtered because of the word of God, and because of the testimony which they had maintained [out of loyalty to Christ]. They cried in a loud voice, saying, "O Lord, holy and true, how long now before You will sit in judgment and avenge our blood on those [unregenerate ones] who dwell on the earth?" Then they were each given a white robe; and they were told to rest and wait quietly for a little while longer, **until the number of their fellow servants and their brothers and sisters who were to be killed even as they had been, would be completed.** *Rev 6:9-11.*

We are getting close to the end of the 6th day according to the Jewish calendar, let's continue doing our Father's business until Jesus returns.

Come Lord Jesus!

Hallelujah!!

CPSIA information can be obtained
at www.ICGtesting.com
Printed in the USA
BVHW091036260722
643029BV00007B/493